BREADS

Delicious loaves and more to bake at home

igloobooks

Published in 2017
by Igloo Books Ltd
Cottage Farm
Sywell
NN6 0BJ
www.igloobooks.com

Original book title: Tuttà la bontà del Pane
© 2013 Gribaudo - IF - Idee editoriali Feltrinelli srl
Socio Unico Giangiacomo Feltrinelli Editore srl
Via Andegari 6 - 20121 Milano
info@gribaudo.it
www.feltrinellieditore.it/gribaudo/

Front cover images: © Rita Maas / Getty Images
Back cover images: © Vincenzo Lonati
Interior images: Vincenzo Lonati, except pages 6-7, 11, 31, 32, 36,
46, 64, 76, 79, 84, 92, 98, 102, 118, 124 (Shutterstock images)

Text by Sara Papa (www.sarapapa.eu)

LEO002 0517
2 4 6 8 10 9 7 5 3 1
ISBN 978-1-78557-250-0

Cover designed by Nicholas Gage
Interiors designed by Simon Parker
Edited by Bobby Newlyn-Jones

Printed and manufactured in China

CONTENTS

RECIPES

WHY MAKE BREAD AT HOME?

Bread, in its many guises, is the most widely eaten food in the world. To talk of bread is to talk of home, family warmth, an act of love performed by whoever makes bread for their loved ones. Its origins are lost in antiquity when, by chance, in Egypt, a ball of flour and water placed beside a fire turned into the first mother dough.

Modern dietitians have reinstated bread to diets, even on the tables of those who have weight and health problems. The reasons that may lead us to prepare homemade bread are simple yet essential: we can choose ingredients of excellent quality, favour natural rising, satisfy every kind of palate and need, create imaginative combinations using the various cereals and enrich our products with seeds and tasty fillings. Well-prepared bread aids the digestion, helping in the protein absorption stage and rendering the gastric juices less acidic. Given that it is a complex carbohydrate, it provides long-lasting and ongoing energy to our bodies.

A further motivation of fundamental importance arises from the fact that in recent years a trend has surfaced among some bakers to make white bread with added fats and other substances that are harmful to our health in order to make them easier to work with and make the bread keep longer. Furthermore, if strong flours are used, the raising times should be extended. However, often this rule is not respected and there is a tendency to shorten the bread-making procedure, thus obtaining indigestible bread and causing an increase in intolerances and allergies.

FLOUR

One of the most important aspects in good bread baking is the use of top quality ingredients: flour is of course one of the most important ingredients. These days we are spoilt for choice with the variety of flours on the market. There really are flours for every recipe, but over recent years there has been an increasing focus on the natural wholesomeness of what we eat: flour plays a fundamental role in this regard. It is important to choose flour carefully as 80% of the success of breadmaking depends on its quality. It is advisable to use flours obtained from ancient grains such as farro and rye. Although they are low in gluten, with the addition of a small percentage of wheat they provide elasticity, strength and stability to the dough and have a good capacity for fermentation; as a result the bread will be more fragrant and tasty.

There are numerous types of flour: the most common is wheat, particularly soft wheat flour, whereas the word "semolina" is used to indicate durum wheat.

There are other flours that are lower in gluten than wheat flour or entirely gluten-free: those are obtained by milling rye, maize and spelt.

By experimenting with combinations of wheat and other flours, you can obtain breads with different appearances, consistencies and flavours. In any case, a small amount of wheat flour should always be used because its protein value favours the development of the gluten necessary for raising. The dough obtained by combining two thirds of wheat flour with one third of flour of another kind allows you to obtain the best results during both the preparation and baking of the bread.

Wholemeal flour is a separate subject. The use of wholegrain cereals has been proven to reduce the risk of cardiovascular diseases, diabetes and cancer; the phytochemical contents, however, such as flavonoids and polyphenols, which are present in the external layers of the grains, are reduced with normal grinding techniques. Therefore, it is necessary to take care when purchasing because there are flours on the market passed off as wholemeal that are actually mixtures of soft white wheat flour and bran. Only grinding with natural stone gives flour these qualities.

WHEAT

This is undoubtedly the most widely used grain. Flour is obtained by grinding the grains, known as caryopses, made up of three elements: bran, endosperm and germ. The bran, which protects the grain, is rich in insoluble fibre, minerals and B vitamins. Inside is the endosperm, the lightest part of the grain. This is mainly made up of starch and proteins, which allow the transformation of the gluten. The majority of refined flours are obtained from the endosperm. The wheat germ is a embryo, therefore it is rich in antioxidants, vitamin E, B vitamins and minerals. The most commonly used varieties for obtaining flour are soft wheat and durum wheat, which contains a greater quantity of protein.

Soft wheat flour is classified based on its level of refinement: the most widely available on the market are soft, plain, strong, very strong and wholemeal. Soft white wheat flour can be distinguished owing to its pure and white appearance, but its nutritional content is very low because to obtain this kind of flour all the external parts of the grain have been eliminated completely. Plain, strong, very strong and wholemeal differ in the level of whole elements extracted from the grain. Strong flour has a percentage of bran, therefore it is less white than plain flour and soft white flour and in very strong flour there is a higher percentage of bran. Wholemeal flour is obtained by grinding the entire grain and contains the highest percentage of bran.

It is important to remember that the quality of the flour depends exclusively on the seed, sowing and soil. It is classified based on its "strength" indicated by the letter W, which indicates its breadmaking capacity, in other words the volume that the dough can reach.

Therefore, there are the following flours:

- weak flours, up to 170 W (suitable for making biscuits, wafers and petit fours); they absorb around 50% of their weight in water.
- medium flours, from 180 to 260 W (for straight dough - or direct dough, bread, and pizza); they absorb from 55% to 65% of their weight in water.
- strong flours, from 280 to 350 W (indirect dough, biga pre-fermentation, naturally risen pastries and pizza); they absorb from 55% to 75% of their weight in water.
- special flours, over 350 W (these are flours made with special grains, above all US and Canadian flours, suitable for preparing types of bread that are difficult to prepare or to strengthen weaker flours); they absorb up to 90% of their weight in water.

DURUM WHEAT

Flour from durum wheat is known as semolina. It is distinct from soft wheat flour owing to its larger granulometry and its characteristic amber yellow colour, which is also found in the products it is used to make. This flour is mainly used for making both fresh and dried pasta. By grinding semolina further, a finer flour is obtained, re-milled semolina, with a finer granulometry than the source product; this product is mainly used for breadmaking and allows the creation of very tasty, yellow bread that keeps well.

RYE

Known from prehistoric times, rye has always been considered a poor man's food. Apparently, it initially grew spontaneously in barley and wheat fields. Its grains are a greyish green in colour and its composition is similar to that of wheat. The flour obtained from it is rich in mineral salts including sodium, potassium and calcium. This flour aids circulation and is considered a good anti-arteriosclerotic.

During the second world war, rye was widely used, given that the wheat was sent to the front to feed the troops. As it is low in gluten, rye flour is mixed with wheat flour in breadmaking. Using natural rising, the result is a highly fragrant, crumbly and non-chewy loaf, with a slight acidic note on the palate.

MAIZE

The origins of this cereal are Central America. It was imported by Christopher Columbus on his return from his travels. In the past, when no other grains were available, a type of bread was made with maize flour called 'de ndianu (Indian bread). It had a heavy consistency, owing to the absence of gluten. It was kneaded in the kneading trough, leaving the dough to rest and, without forming it into a loaf shape, when the wood-burning oven was hot enough, it was picked up with a bowl, placed on the floured wooden pizza paddle and then slid into the oven for baking. Maize flour is lower in protein than that of other cereals.

STARCH AND GLUTEN

Starch is a complex carbohydrate (sugar), made up of glucose molecules. It has an important role in kneading because it absorbs the water. It transforms into fermenting sugars, essential for raising and giving the characteristic brown colour to the bread. Gluten is a lipoprotein created by the combination of two types of protein - gliadin and glutenin - together with water. This makes the doughs sticky, elastic and cohesive. The quantity and quality of gluten present in a flour are an important indication in order to assess the quality and capacity for breadmaking. In soft wheat flour, the minimum quantity of dry gluten is 7%. Generally speaking, all other factors being equal, the greater the gluten content, the better the quality of the end product. When dough is formed with flour and water, the gluten creates an internal grid structure that captures the gases produced during the raising phase and allows the dough to increase in volume, taking on an elastic consistency.

SPELT

Famous for being the staple of the Roman legions, Spelt was mainly used to prepare bread, focaccia and polenta. Spelt is an undemanding plant, resistant to adverse weather conditions and parasite attacks. However, its cultivation has gradually been reduced over the course of the centuries, having been replaced by soft wheat (a descendent of large spelt) and durum wheat (a descendent of medium spelt), with a greater yield and lower processing costs. Rich in protein, minerals and vitamins, spelt is particularly good as a restorative and excellent for the preparation of soups. In breadmaking, its flour can be mixed with wheat and rye flours.

RAISING AGENTS

A crucial point for making the most of the characteristics of each type flour is the choice of raising agent. Yeast is a unicellular microorganism that breathes, reproduces and, like all living organisms, needs an ideal environment for their activity. The term yeast therefore refers to a colony of microscopic funghi, present in large quantities in plants, fruits and the air itself.

It is calculated that in one gram of yeast there are around 80 billion cells, which are able to make even a mineral substance absorbable with their activity. In breadmaking, the purpose of the yeast is to make the dough ferment, increasing its volume, through the transformation of the sugars and development of carbon dioxide and alcohol; these processes make the bread light, digestible and easy to absorb.

These days raising agents can be classified in three categories:

- Chemical raising agents;
- Compressed or brewer's yeast;
- Pre-ferment or mother dough.

CHEMICAL RAISING AGENTS

These are substances obtained by means of chemical processes; sodium bicarbonate, cream of tartar and ammonium bicarbonate belong to this category. These react at 100°C, generating carbon dioxide, which is what provokes the increase in volume of the mixture. When using this kind of raising agent, it is not necessary to leave the dough to rise. Chemical raising agents are not normally used for breadmaking so are, therefore, not used for the recipes in this book.

COMPRESSED OR BREWER'S YEAST

This yeast is mainly obtained from a Saccaromyces Cerevisiae culture. The name is derived from the fact that, at one time, it was extracted from the residue from brewing beer. It would be more appropriate to call it compressed yeast, as it no longer has anything to do with brewing beer and is produced industrially from the fermentation of molasses, a by-product of beet sugar. Sold in blocks of 25 g, it is greyish-white in colour and has an acidic, slightly aromatic odour. In order to develop carbon dioxide, it needs time (at least thirty minutes) and a temperature of around 22-23°C. Before being added to the flour, it must be crumbled and dissolved in slightly tepid water (no hotter than 25°C, because excessive heat, just like the cold, renders it inactive). This is the yeast used in the industry, given that it is an extremely powerful fermenting agent, meaning that it permits rapid breadmaking. It is highly perishable, leading to a loss of its organoleptic characteristics and a lessening of its fermenting power. To get around these drawbacks, the industry also produces dried yeast, which, given that it is dehydrated, has a low humidity content (around 8%). It is far more stable and can be stored for a long time in a fresh environment or even frozen. Before use, it must be reactivated in water at 37-38°C (if it is instant, on the other hand, it can be mixed directly with the ingredients).

One gram of dried yeast is equivalent to 3 g of fresh yeast. Generally speaking, this kind of yeast is sold in 7-8 g packets, so one packet is the equivalent of one 25 g block of brewer's yeast. It can be kept for six months or vacuum packed for up to two years. It may be useful to know the conversion factor between brewer's yeast and dried yeast:

1 g fresh brewer's yeast x 0.4	=	1 g dried yeast
1 g dried yeast x 2.5	=	1 g fresh brewer's yeast
1 g instant dried yeast x 1.5	=	1 g fresh brewer's yeast

MOTHER DOUGH

Also known as sourdough starter, this is "the mother of all yeast". Bacteria and funghi are normally found in the air and on every surface. In the presence of a flour and water dough, these microorganisms give rise to fermentation, transforming the sugars into starch.

In mother dough, in addition to saccharomycetales, there are also lactobacillusm, the bacteria responsible for the transformation of sugar into lactic acid and, as a result, the souring of the dough. Therefore, in natural rising together with alcoholic fermentation, performed by the saccharomycetales, an acid fermentation takes place, which gives the bread a particular taste and aroma.

The micro flora of a mother dough is never the same but varies according to the breadmaking conditions and raw materials used. We can say that the micro flora that will be obtained by mixing flour and water will depend on:

• Microorganisms present in the grains (and therefore in the flour)
• Microorganisms present in the water
• Microorganisms present in the environment

The use of mother dough rather than brewer's yeast leads to:

• Greater acidity of the bread, which will keep well
• A more uniformly porous crumb structure, owing to its gradual fermentation
• A slightly sour flavour and aroma
• Better digestibility
• Destruction of the phytic acid. These compounds are present particularly in whole grain wheat flour and prevent iron, calcium and zinc absorption; furthermore they neutralise certain digestive enzymes. The acidity of the dough "destroys" these substances.

From a certain point of view, the preparation of a mother dough is simple because all you need to do is mix flour and water to obtain fermentation. However, it is a delicate operation that requires care and patience. To create and obtain a good mother dough, you will need to wait for at least a month. During this period, the dough will become sour because the microorganisms present in the environment will transform the sugars of the flour into starch, carbon dioxide and other elements.

Mother dough must be obtained using flour and water. To reduce the production times, some bakers recommend adding overripe fruit, yogurt or honey to the mixture. Others suggest vinegar, grappa or aniseed to increase the speed of acidification.

BENEFICIAL RISING!

The presence of a particular saccharomycetales (Saccaromices Elypsoideus) in mother dough helps us to maintain the biological balance of our digestive system and to fight off various intestinal pathogenic germs, such as salmonella, for example. With the natural rising in sourdough, bacteria and yeast are balanced and perform a sort of pre-digestion of the flour, aiding its proper absorption by our bodies. It is always preferable to consume the bread the day after it is made as it is only after resting that it really reveals the full depth of its aromas.

PREPARING MOTHER DOUGH

INGREDIENTS FOR 300 G OF MOTHER DOUGH

- 200 g / 7 oz / 1 ⅓ cups strong stone ground flour
- 100ml / 3 ½ fl oz / ⅓ cup water

Mix the flour with the water until it is no longer sticky. Form the dough into a ball and leave it to rest in a container, ideally a glass container, covered with a damp cloth in a covered place for around 48 hours or until it starts to rise. The rising time depends on the type of flour used and the room temperature. Once 48 hours have passed, you will need to do a series of feedings, adding flour to the mother dough already made (the same kind of flour used for the original dough and the same amount as the weight of the mother dough) and then adding water (around 50% of the weight of the mother dough: the proportion varies depending on the type of flour). Therefore, if your sourdough starter weighs 200 g, you will need 200 g of flour and 100 g of water. During these steps, so that you do not end up with too much yeast, it is recommend that around half of the mother dough is thrown away before each feeding. At this point, your mother dough is ready for breadmaking.

For a kilogram of dough, you will need 150-200 g of mother dough. To make the bread, you dissolve it in warm water and prepare a paste, adding part of the flour (around 200 g but you can make a rough guess). Then knead it and leave it to rest overnight. The next day, add the remaining flour and other ingredients to the risen mixture and start kneading. At this point, before forming the loaf, all you need to do is set aside a piece of dough from the breadmaking to have mother dough available for the future occasions. However, this can only be done if the dough has not been "contaminated" by ingredients such as fats, seeds and special flours. In such cases, it is best to separate your mother dough before adding them.

The mother dough can be kept for a week in a sealed container in the fridge as it will slowly lose its fermenting power. Once fed, it will serve as the mother dough for the next breadmaking session. If you do not have the opportunity to bake bread often, the mother dough must nevertheless be fed because, as time passes, the acid bacteria get the upper hand over the alcoholic bacteria (saccharomycetales, those mainly responsible for bread rising) and, as a result, the bread does not rise very much and is too sour. To get around this problem, you need to stimulate and revitalise the alcoholic fermentation fairly frequently by feeding the dough. At least every 4-5 days, you should mix the mother dough with more flour and water (always the same amount used for the original dough; all you need to do is choose good quality stone ground flour) to create a new loaf. This process will increase the number of saccharomycetales, which are responsible for eliminating the acid bacteria. As a result, a good way of maintaining the yeast active is, of course, making bread often. If you do not manage to feed the dough as often as recommended, there is no need to worry: the yeast stays alive for a week. If more days pass, you can use it all the same; you will just need to use a lesser quantity with a greater quantity of flour. Alternatively, you can feed it a number of times to reduce the acidity.

Often, the mother dough can be passed between various relatives and friends. This allows the use of a tried and tested, effective mother dough, without having to prepare it every time.

STORING MOTHER DOUGH

For the best storage of the mother dough, wrap it in a clean cloth and tie it up, without tying it too tight. It can be kept at room temperature for 12 hours. This type of storage is also common in professional settings. Alternatively, you can keep it in the fridge, either tied up in a cloth or in a little pot; this will slow the fermentation process. A mother dough tied up in a cloth sours more slowly and ensures optimal production, whereas one left open will consume the sugars in half the time. In both cases, a crust will form on the dough. To make bread, you will need to throw it away and only use the inner part of the dough.

To avoid losing the mother dough by forgetting about it, you can keep 200 g in the freezer, after having kept it in the fridge for a few hours. To defrost it, place it back in the fridge for a while and then do two feedings close together to get its strength back. Alternatively, you can dry it, placing mother dough and flour in equal quantities in a mixer. Leave the powder created to dry on a cloth and then keep it in a bag in the fridge.

WATER, SALT, OIL...

While flour is the base to make bread, other ingredients are also necessary. Although these other ingredients are less important in percentage terms, they must be selected and treated with equal care because they affect the final result.

LIQUIDS

When water is mixed with flour, it causes the starch to swell and activates the formation of gluten. The ideal temperature of the dough is around 25°C. To achieve this, it is important to assess what temperature the liquid added to the flour should be. Hence, in the winter, the water should be hotter than in the summer. By way of example, if the ingredients in the room are at 20°C, the water added must have a temperature of around 30°C.

In many recipes in which water is used, no precise temperature is specified, only referring to warm water; this is the case for bread too. It can therefore be useful to fall back on the empirical rule of 70 to establish the correct temperature of the water. According to this rule, the sum of the temperature of flour, air and water must be 70°C. If the room temperature is 20°C, the flour must be at a similar temperature, usually one degree lower, therefore:

room temperature:	20°C
flour temperature:	19°C
water temperature:	31°C
total :	70°C

Therefore the water must be just tepid, more cold than hot. Without having to resort to using thermometers, you can simply make a rough guess, taking into account that if it is a bit colder, the water must be slightly warmer, whereas, if it is very hot, cooler water can be used. This little trick should allow you to obtain a good dough with less effort.

Generally speaking, it is preferable to use fairly hard water but water that is too hard tends to be too slow rising, whereas water that is too soft makes the dough sticky. The water in our homes, owing to the laws on chlorinated water, is not particularly suitable for breadmaking. In order to eliminate undesirable volatile compounds (such as chloride and calcium salts), water should be boiled before use.

In order to obtain bread with a very soft crumb, you can replace part of the water with milk. If, on the other hand, you use yogurt, you will obtain an almost moist consistency, more similar to that of a cake. Generally speaking, it is a good idea to always keep to the amounts of liquids indicated in the recipes, because their ratio to the flour is fundamental.

SALT

Sodium chloride is an important element in the dough as it acts on the composition of gluten. A dough to which no salt has been added tends to be gluey, white and sticky. In the rising phase, salt slows fermentation, reduces the development of gases and tends to give the bread a finer crumb. It should be measured carefully because, given that it has a pH that is slightly alkaline, it works against the action of the yeast.

Salt makes the bread keep longer, makes it crustier and makes the crust brown better. Bear in mind that a change in the amount of salt has a significant effect on the reactions of the dough, therefore, you should always weigh it, to ensure that the end product is consistent. The recommended amount is 2-2.5% of the weight of the flour. Furthermore, salt should never be added to the dough together with the yeast as it would damage its properties. Ideally fine sea salt should be used as it is less alkaline.

FATS

These are the first ingredients used for breadmaking, following the basic ones described above, and they change the structure of the dough, creating an oily layer between the gluten proteins and the starch particles. The dough will become more elastic and have a greater volume. The most commonly used fats are butter, lard and vegetable oils while the most digestible of all the fats is undoubtedly extra virgin olive oil. By contrast to other vegetable oils - rich in polyunsaturated fatty acids that are unstable when heated and therefore, above certain temperatures produce substances that are toxic for the liver - extra virgin olive oil has a far more balanced polyunsaturated fat content and is more suitable for use in cooking.

Fats affect rising significantly. Solid fats particularly, if added in small amounts (2-5% of the total weight of the dough), can improve the structure of the gluten and therefore increase the volume of the finished product. Larger amounts do not help rising as they make the dough heavy, although they do make it softer, more crumbly and moister. In recipes with a high fat content, it is a good idea to add the fats only at the end of kneading. If the fat is added at the beginning, it tends to form a film around the grains of starch that prevent the gluten hydrating well.

MALT

This compound is derived from the germination of grains (barley, wheat, rice, etc.). It is one of the main ingredients in the preparation of many types of bread and its action helps to stimulate fermentation, gives colour and flavour to the bread and creates a better risen end product. If you do not have malt, you can use acacia honey.

DOUGHS

The methods of making dough can be divided into three groups: the direct method, the semi-direct method and the indirect method. The first method is undoubtedly the easiest one. All you need to do is mix all of the ingredients together; the bread obtained is nevertheless less tasty and does not keep as well.

In the semi-direct method, you add mother dough to the dough or a piece of risen dough from the preceding day, kept covered with a damp cloth: the bread obtained has intense and slightly sour flavours and aromas and can be kept for a few days. The indirect method involves adding dough from a risen mixture in which there is already active yeast present. There are several advantages to this method: the distribution of the yeast in the mixture is more uniform, the dough is better aerated, crusty and easier to digest. The mixtures that can be added in the indirect method are biga, poolish and lievitino.

BIGA

This is a dry dough made of flour, water and yeast: an amount of water is used equal to 45% of the weight of the flour and an amount of yeast equal to 1%. Once prepared, biga is used in the final dough the next day. To make this type of dough, a very strong flour is required.

To make biga, knead 300 g / 10 ½ oz of strong flour with 3 g of yeast dissolved in 140 ml / 5 fl oz / ⅔ cups of cold water for a few minutes. Leave the ball of dough, covered, at 16-18 °C for 18-24 hours, or place it in the fridge at 4-6 °C for 36-48 hours, taking it out and leaving it at room temperature for the last hours of rising. Biga is used in a percentage of 40-50% of the amount of flour indicated in the recipe.

POOLISH

By contrast to biga, poolish is a soft and fast-acting mixture. It is obtained by mixing water, flour and yeast in proportions to obtain a very liquid dough: the water to flour ratio is 1:1.

To make poolish, mix 300 g / 10 ½ oz of flour in a bowl with 1g of yeast dissolved in 300 ml / 10 ½ fl oz / 1 ¼ cups of cold water. Leave the mixture to rise at 16-18°C for 6-8 hours. To reduce the times, you can double the amount of yeast or leave the mixture to rise at 22°C / 70F.

Poolish is used in a percentage of about 20-30% of the amount of flour indicated in the recipe. Its characteristic is that the percentage of yeast varies based on the duration of fermentation:

- 2.5% of the weight of flour for a fermentation of 2 hours
- 1.5% of the weight of flour for a fermentation of 3 hours
- 0.5% of the weight of flour for a fermentation of 8 hours
- 0.1% of the weight of flour for a fermentation of 16 hours

LIEVITINO

This is a simple and rapid pre-ferment that accelerates the rising process without giving the bread particular aromas and flavours. It is left to rest until it doubles in volume, usually about an hour, and involves the use of the entire amount of brewer's yeast in the recipe. To obtain the right amount of prove, mix together ⅓ of the total flour in the recipe, 50% of the water calculated based on one third of the flour and all the yeast in the recipe. The amount of water used for the lievitino must then be subtracted from the amount shown for the remaining mixture.

PIZZA

Universally enjoyed, pizza can be interpreted in a thousand different ways. Enhance pizzas with savoury toppings such as fresh tomato, buffalo mozzarella and basil or thin slices of aubergine, mozzarella and chilli oil. Sweet toppings are equally delicious: sliced figs, toasted almonds and rounds of banana, chocolate sauce, walnuts or even slices of pineapple, honey and crumbled amaretti can be added once cooked. By changing the ingredients for the toppings, you can make pizzas in line with seasonal produce.

PREPARING PIZZA DOUGH (SERVES 6 PEOPLE)

FOR THE POOLISH

- 100 g strong stone ground flour / 3 ½ oz / ⅔ cup
- 100 ml water / 3 ⅓ fl oz / ⅓ cups
- 0.5g brewer's yeast

FOR THE DOUGH

- 500 g flour / 17 ½ oz / 3 ⅓ cups
- 10 g brewer's yeast
- 250 ml water / 8 ¾ fl oz / 1 cup
- 20 ml extra virgin olive oil
- pinch salt
- 1 tbsp re-milled durum wheat semolina

1. To make the poolish: in a bowl, mix the flour, water and yeast into a sticky mixture. Cover the bowl with cling film and leave to rise overnight.

2. The next morning, prepare the dough. Sieve the flour onto a work surface, form a well in the centre and pour in the yeast dissolved in the water.

3. Mix part of the liquid into the flour with a fork then add the oil, salt and poolish.

4. Knead until you have a smooth, elastic dough. Place it in an oiled bowl, cover with cling film and leave to rise until it doubles in volume.

5. Turn the bowl upside down on a work surface sprinkled with durum wheat semolina so that the dough detaches from the bowl and falls out slowly. With your fingertips, extend the dough to form a rectangle with a thickness of one centimetre.

6. Transfer the rectangular dough to a baking tray lined with greaseproof paper and sprinkle with more semolina, extending it uniformly with your fingertips.

7. Top the pizza as desired then place the baking tray in the oven, preheated to 220°C / 430F. Place it at the bottom of the oven for 10 minutes so that it forms a crust then place in the middle of the oven to finish cooking for another 25-30 minutes.

FILO PASTRY

Phyllo in Greek means 'leaf'. This is a kind of pastry prepared in very fine separate sheets. Traditionally, it is used throughout the Middle East to make sweets stuffed with walnuts and pistachios and submerged in a sugar and spice syrup, like a baklava. The artesanal technique for its preparation is very spectacular.

Filo pastry cooks very quickly, either baked in the oven or fried to prepare all sorts of haute cuisine dishes and replaces the casing of various rolls in many different cuisines around the world. By contrast to normal puff pastry, it is produced without the addition of butter; its neutral flavour allows it to be used with both sweet and savoury dishes.

PREPARING FILO PASTRY

- 250 g soft wheat flour / 8 ¾ oz / 1 ⅔ cups
- 150 ml warm water / 5 ⅓ fl oz / ⅔ cup
- a pinch of salt
- extra virgin olive oil

1. Sieve the flour onto the pastry board and make a well in the centre. Mix it with the water and salt until you have a soft and smooth dough. Form it into a ball, cover with a damp cloth and leave to rest for about half an hour.

2. Divide the dough into balls of around 40-50 g / 1 ½-1 ¾ oz each and roll them out with a long rolling pin to about 2 cm (1 in) in diameter, with a minimum length of 80 cm (31 in), until you have lots of discs that are just a few millimetres thick.

3. Take the first disc of dough and grease it with a little oil. Place a second disc of dough on top [3a] and grease again [3b]. Cover with a third disc [3c] and, with a rolling pin, press down repeatedly on the three discs first lengthwise and then crosswise, as if to form a lattice [3d, 3e].

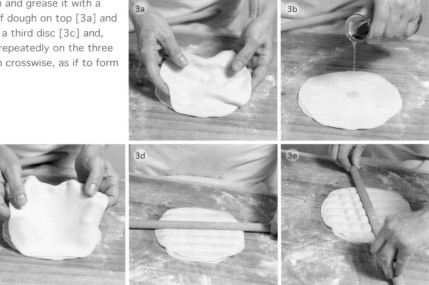

4. Start to roll out the pastry, flouring it if necessary. Wrap the pastry around the rolling pin [4a] and unroll it quickly with a decisive movement of the wrists [4b]. You should get a very fine sheet of pastry. Arrange the pastry on a cloth and continue as indicated in points 3 and 4 with the remaining pastry, until you have used it all up.

5. You can make filo pastry with more than three discs. For filo pastry to be used in sweets, five or more discs are laid on top of each other.

EQUIPMENT

To make bread at home, there are some tools you will need, as listed below. Almost all of them are found in any kitchen. Some of them you can do with out, using different methods instead but, ideally, if you want to produce homemade bread on an ongoing basis, you should have them all to hand.

Mixers, in particular, are useful for mixing the ingredients and kneading the dough. The ideal procedure would be to knead it by hand on a pastry board but if you do not have much time, you can take advantage of a mixer. However, it is important to take care because some mixers heat the dough too much, which may put the success of your loaf at risk. Rolling pins should also be used with care: they are useful for rolling out unrisen dough but should be used as little as possible for rolling out doughs with yeast, for which it is preferable to work with your hands.

THINGS YOU WILL NEED TO MAKE BREAD

- Pastry board
- Mixer
- Rolling pin
- Scraper or spatula for diving the dough
- Various loaf tins for sandwich bread
- Bowls of various sizes
- Containers for rising
- Pastry brush

- Sieve
- Kitchen thermometer
- Tea towels
- Kitchen scales
- Greaseproof paper and cling film
- Cooling rack
- Oven

BEFORE YOU BEGIN: A FEW TIPS...

- Some of the following recipes provide the amount of both brewer's yeast and mother dough. It is up to you to decide which to use. Mother dough Is the best, but if you decide to use it, remember to increase the rising times in relation to those shown in the recipe.

- It is sensible to reduce these times by increasing the amount of mother dough.

- Be careful about how you store flour. Once purchased, it is best to put it in a dry place with no humidity, far from any heat sources.

- To know when the dough has risen and is ready for cooking, you need to take out a little ball of dough (before shaping the loaf!) and put it in a glass of very cold water. If the little ball floats to the top, the dough has risen.

- If you want to use brewer's yeast, make lievitino the evening before with 2 g of brewer's yeast, 120 ml / 4 ¼ fl oz of water and 220 g / 7 ¾ fl oz of flour. The following morning mix it with the ingredients in the recipe.

- If you do not have kitchen scales, try not to worry about the weight of the ingredients. The important thing is that the final dough is compact and smooth. If it is too hard, add water. If it is too soft, add flour.

- Always choose top quality ingredients.

- Always sieve the flour, except whole grain flour. Sieving flour oxygenates it, which will make your bread softer.

- All of the ingredients that make up a recipe must be at room temperature.
- Doughs with mother dough have longer rising times than those with brewer's yeast.
- Usually, the amount of mother dough necessary for a kilo of flour is 150 g.
- When the dough has risen, it must be baked immediately. Do not wait, otherwise it will deflate and collapse.
- Always flour greaseproof paper and the top of more rustic loaves with flour of the same kind as the one used for the dough. The flour on the baking tray will absorb part of the humidity of the bread and the flour on top will create a warmer colour as it bakes.
- In domestic ovens, avoid using the fan function as it dries the outside too much and cooks the inside less.
- To achieve the right level of moistness when baking, you can place 5-6 ice cubes in the bottom of the oven just before putting the loaf in the oven: they will melt immediately, creating the necessary steam to make the crusts of more delicate loaves softer.
- Never open the oven in the first 20-25 minutes of baking, to avoid affecting the rising process.
- Do not throw away leftover bread. You can reuse it as breadcrumbs, or toasted as bruschetta.

RECIPES

TRADITIONAL WHITE BREAD

- 600 g / 21 oz / 3 ⅔ cups strong flour
- 12 g brewer's yeast or 150 g / 5 ⅓ oz / 1 cup mother dough
- 350 ml / 12 ⅓ fl oz / 1 ½ cups water
- 1 teaspoon salt
- extra virgin olive oil

1. Dissolve the yeast in the water at a temperature of 22-23°C / 70-73F until it has dissolved completely. Place the sieved flour on the pastry board, forming a well in the centre, pour in the dissolved yeast and begin to combine. Add the salt and knead until the dough is smooth and compact. Place the dough in a large oiled bowl and cover with a damp cloth, placing it somewhere where it is not in a draught. Leave it to rise until it has doubled in volume.

2. Knead the dough, shaping it into a long roll, and transfer it to a baking tray lined with greaseproof paper. With a sharp knife, score the surface of the bread creating a lattice pattern. Leave to rest in a warm place until it has risen again.

3. Bake in a preheated oven at 210-220°C / 400-425F for 15 minutes, then reduce the temperature to 180°C / 350F and bake for a further 35 minutes. After baking, leave the bread to cool on a cooling rack.

PERFECT WITH...

This bread is perfect with red chilli chutney. Clean and chop 5 red chillis and 300 g of red bell pepper. Peel and grate 3 cm of fresh ginger. Very gently fry in 20 g of extra virgin olive oil, one onion and a clove of garlic. Add the ginger, pepper, chilli, 250 g sugar and half a teaspoon of salt. Cook for 30 minutes, blend and leave to cool in sterilised jars.

FILONCINO
ITALIAN-STYLE BAGUETTE WITH DURUM WHEAT SEMOLINA

- 600 g / 21 oz / 3 ⅔ cups re-milled durum wheat semolina
- 12 g brewer's yeast or 150 g / 5 ⅓ oz / 1 cup mother dough
- 400 ml / 14 fl oz / 1 ⅔ cups water
- 1 tsp acacia honey (or malt)
- 10 g salt

1. Dissolve the yeast in water at room temperature. Add the sieved flour and knead for 3 or 4 minutes, then add the honey and salt until you have an elastic, smooth dough. Shape the bread into a baguette shape and transfer to a floured baking tray. With a serrated knife, make some diagonal scores of about 1 cm (½ in) in depth.

2. Cover the bread with a tea towel and leave it to rise until it has doubled in size. Bake in a preheated oven for 15 minutes at 220°C / 425F, then reduce the temperature to 180°C / 350F and bake for a further 35 minutes. Take it out of the oven and leave the loaf to cool on a cooling rack.

A TIP...
For this recipe, use re-milled durum wheat semolina for breadmaking and not the normal durum wheat semolina, which is only suitable for homemade pasta. Re-milled semolina has a finer grain and is therefore more suitable for breadmaking.

GERMAN BREAD

- 1 kg / 35 ¼ oz / 7 cups whole grain flour
- 570 ml / 20 fl oz / 2 ⅓ cups water
- 300 g / 10 ½ oz / 2 cups mother dough
- 30 ml extra virgin olive oil
- 20 g chestnut honey
- 30 g toasted sesame seeds

- 30 g flax seeds
- 40 g cups sunflower seeds (or pumpkin seeds)
- 20 g cups salt
- mixed seeds for decoration

1. Dissolve the mother dough in warm water (22-23°C / 71-73F). Make a well in the flour, add the yeast mixture and mix with a fork. Add the oil, honey, seeds and salt. Knead for 4-5 minutes until you have a soft, smooth dough. Leave the dough to rest for 20 minutes in an oiled bowl covered with a sheet of cling film.

2. Sprinkle the seeds for decoration onto the pastry board, gently turn out the dough and roll it so that it is completely covered in seeds. Shape the bread to make it round or into a baguette shape and place it on a baking tray lined with greaseproof paper. With a sharp knife, make some diagonal scores of about 1 cm (½ in) deep. Leave the bread until it has doubled in volume. Bake it for 15 minutes in a preheated oven at 220°C / 425F, then bake for 45 minutes at 180°C / 350F. Take the loaf out of the oven and leave it to cool on a cooling rack.

CIABATTA WITH POOLISH

FOR THE POOLISH

- 300 g / 10 ½ oz / 2 cups strong flour
- 300 ml / 10 ½ fl oz / 1 ¼ cups water
- 7.5 g brewer's yeast or 95 g / 3 ⅓ oz / ¾ cup mother dough

FOR THE DOUGH

- 600 g / 21 oz / 4 cups strong flour
- 375 ml / 13 ¼ fl oz / 1 ½ cups water
- 9 g brewer's yeast or 113 g / 4 oz / ¾ cup mother dough
- 9 g malt
- 18 g salt
- extra virgin olive oil
- re-milled durum wheat semolina

1. To make the poolish: dissolve the yeast in water (at around 22°C / 71F). Add the sieved flour and knead by hand. Leave to rise at room temperature for 2 hours.

2. To make the dough: place the flour, malt and salt in a large bowl. Dilute the yeast in the water and pour the mixture obtained onto the poolish. Combine and pour into the flour bowl. Knead, flouring your hands but without adding any more flour to the dough, which must be soft. Pour into an oiled container and leave to rest for about an hour.

3. Turn the container upside down on a work surface sprinkled with semolina. Dust the surface of the dough with semolina. Break up the dough, cutting strips that are 5 cm (2 in) in width by about 10 cm (4 in) in length. Place them on the pastry board with the cut part uppermost, flatten the little ciabbatas with your fingertips, stretch them slightly and ease them onto the baking tray lined with floured greaseproof paper. Leave to rise until they have doubled in volume, covering them with a tea towel to avoid them forming a crust.

4. Place an oven-proof dish with 5-6 ice cubes on the bottom of the oven to create steam. Bake in an oven preheated to 220°C / 425F for about 20 minutes.

PERFECT WITH...

This ciabatta is excellent with a hazelnut chocolate spread. Chop 300 g of 55% cocoa dark chocolate and melt it over a bain marie at 45-50°C. Add 400 g condensed milk, 150 g hazelnut paste and 150 g fresh milk added in a slow steady trickle. Remove from the heat and stir until the spread becomes velvety. Leave to cool and store in the fridge.

DURUM WHEAT FLOWER

FOR THE BIGA

- 250 g / 8 ¾ oz / 1 ⅔ cups strong flour
- 115 ml / 4 fl oz / 2 cups water
- 2.5 g brewer's yeast or 30 g mother dough

FOR THE DOUGH

- 750 g / 26 ½ oz / 5 cups re-milled durum wheat semolina
- 500 ml / 17 ½ oz / 2 cups water
- 15 g brewer's yeast or 190 g / 6 ¾ oz / 1 ⅓ cups mother dough
- 10 g malt
- 15 g salt
- extra virgin olive oil

1. For the biga, make a smooth, elastic dough with water, flour and yeast, kneading it for about 3 minutes. Leave the resulting biga to rise for 12 hours, covered with a sheet of cling film.

2. For the dough, mix the biga with the dough dissolved in the water, the malt and the semolina and start to knead. Halfway through kneading, add the salt, then continue to knead until the dough is smooth and compact. Place the dough in an oiled bowl, cover it with a tea towel and leave to rise for about an hour.

A TIP...

For a perfect result, once cooked, remove the durum wheat flower from the baking tray, turn the oven off, then place it back in the hot oven and leave it there until the oven has cooled completely.

3. Break up the dough and shape into round loaves weighing about 400 g / 14 oz each [3a]. To shape each one into a flower, sink your fingers into the centre of each loaf [3b] and form a raised middle of the flower, then fold the outer parts inwards to form the petals [3c, 3d]. Dust the loaves with plenty of semolina, score a cross in the centre of the flower [3e], then gently place the flowers on a baking tray lined with greaseproof paper and leave them to rise at a temperature of 28°C / 82F until they have doubled in volume.

4. Bake in the oven preheated to 220°C / 425F for 30 minutes, placing 4 or 5 ice cubes in the oven to create steam. Reduce the temperature to 180°C / 350F and continue to bake for another 10 minutes.

MILK AND WALNUT SANDWICH LOAF

- 500 g / 17 ¾ oz / 3 ⅓ cups strong flour
- 260 ml / 9 fl oz / 1 cup whole milk
- 120 g / 4 ¼ oz / 1 ½ cups walnut kernels
- 12 g brewer's yeast or 150 g / 5 ¼ oz / 1 cup mother dough
- 1 tsp malt or honey
- 10 g salt
- extra virgin olive oil
- butter
- 1 egg yolk
- milk

1. Dissolve the yeast in around 50 ml / 1 ¾ fl. oz of warm milk, then knead the mixture obtained with 100 g / 3 ½ oz flour. Shape it into a ball, place in a bowl, cover with a cloth and leave to rise for about 30 minutes in a warm place.

2. Once the time is up, place the remaining sieved flour in a mound on the pastry board, forming a well in the centre. Place the raised dough, malt, salt and remaining milk in the well. Combine and add the chopped walnuts. Knead until you have a soft but firm mixture. Place it in an oiled bowl and leave it to rise for about 40 minutes.

3. Pour the dough onto the pasty board, divide it into three equal parts and plait it, joining the two ends. Gently place the plait in a 28 cm (11 in) loaf tin, lined with greaseproof paper. Leave the bread to rise in a warm place until it has doubled in volume.

4. Brush the top of the plait with the egg yolk diluted with a drop of milk and bake in a preheated oven at 180°C / 350F for 55 minutes. Once baked, turn off the oven, take the plait out of the tin, place it on a cooling rack and place it back in the hot oven until it cools.

A TIP...

If you are lactose intolerant, you can replace the cow's milk with rice milk, soy milk or water.

MINI WHOLEMEAL FOCACCIAS

- 650 g / 23 oz / 4 ⅓ cups whole grain flour
- 12 g brewer's yeast or 150 g / 5 ¼ oz / 1 ¼ cups mother dough
- 300 ml / 10 ½ fl oz / 1 ¼ cups water
- 50 g / 1 ¾ oz / ¼ cups honey
- 30 ml / 1 fl oz / 1 cup extra virgin olive oil
- 1 teaspoon salt

1. Dissolve the yeast with water and honey, add the flour, begin kneading, then add the salt dissolved in a drop of water. Knead again and add the oil. Knead again until you have a smooth and elastic dough, place it in an oiled bowl, cover with a sheet of cling film and leave to rise until it doubles in volume.

2. Gently turn the dough out onto a floured pastry board and spread it out with your hands, cut out the focaccias with a round pastry cutter with a diameter of about 10 cm (4 in). Place them on a baking tray lined with greaseproof paper and leave to rise for 15-20 minutes, then bake them in a preheated oven at 190°C / 375F for about 20 minutes.

WHOLE GRAIN FLOUR

By nature, this flour has a variable consistency that can absorb more or less water. Therefore, you will always need to check the proportions of the ingredients, increasing the amounts of flour and water if necessary.

CHAPATIS

- 500 g / 17 ⅔ oz / 3 ⅓ cups strong flour
- 250 ml / 8 3/4 fl oz / 1 cups water
- tsp salt

1. Make a well in the centre of the flour, add the salt, pour the water into the centre and knead. Leave the dough to rest for 10 minutes, covered with a tea towel. Divide the dough into lots of little balls of the same weight. Roll out the dough evenly with a rolling pin: the result should be similar to little, thin pizzas, each with a diameter of 15 cm (6 in).

2. Heat a heavy-bottomed, non-stick pan over a medium heat; when it is nice and hot, place one of the chapatis on it and cook over a low heat for a few minutes; turn it over and leave to cook for a few minutes more. Turn it over again and it will swell up almost like a balloon. These steps are very important to ensure that the chapatis are a success. Once you have cooked the first chapati, put it on a plate and cover with a tea towel to keep it warm. Continue like this until you have used up all the dough.

QUICK AND DELICIOUS

This recipe is an excellent option if you want bread that is ready immediately, without the need for rising and long baking. Chapatis are also suitable for those with yeast intolerance and for those who prefer to eat unleavened bread. Excellent variations can be created using wholemeal flour or strong flour.

RAINBOW LOAF

FOR THE WHITE DOUGH BASE

- 150 g / 5 ⅓ oz / 1 cup strong flour
- 75 ml / 2 ⅔ fl oz / ⅓ cup water
- 1 tsp honey or sugar
- 6 g brewer's yeast or 75 g / 2 ⅔ oz / ½ cup mother dough
- 1 tsp extra virgin olive oil
- 2 g salt

FOR THE RED DOUGH

- 120 g / 4 ¼ oz / ¾ cup strong flour
- 50 g / 1 ¾ oz / ¼ cup tomato paste or puree
- 30 g sweet paprika
- 25 ml water
- 1 tsp honey or sugar
- 6 g brewer's yeast or 75 g / 2 ⅔ oz / ½ cup mother dough
- 1 tsp extra virgin olive oil
- 2 g salt

FOR THE GREEN DOUGH

- 150 g / 5 ⅓ oz / 1 cup strong flour
- 200 g / 7 oz / 3 cups raw spinach leaves
- 100 ml / 3 ½ fl oz / ½ cup water
- 1 tsp honey or sugar
- 6 g brewer's yeast or 75 g / 2 ⅔ oz / ½ cup mother dough
- 1 tsp extra virgin olive oil
- 2 g salt

FOR THE YELLOW DOUGH

- 130 g / 4 ½ oz / ¾ cup strong flour
- 20 g turmeric
- 1 sachet of saffron or 75 g water
- 1 tsp honey or sugar
- 6 g brewer's yeast or 75 g / 2 ⅔ oz / ½ cup mother dough
- 1 tsp extra virgin olive oil
- 2 g salt

FOR THE BLACK DOUGH

- 150 g / 5 ⅓ oz / 1 cup strong flour
- 5 g squid ink
- 75 ml / 2 ⅔ fl oz / ⅓ cup water
- 1 tsp of honey or sugar
- 6 g brewer's yeast or 75 g / 2 ⅔ oz / ½ cup mother dough
- 1 tsp extra virgin olive oil
- 2 g salt

FOR BRUSHING

- 2 egg yolks

PERFECT WITH...

This colourful and very aromatic bread is particularly good with cured meats and cheeses and for making crostini with fish toppings.

1. To make this loaf, you will need to make five doughs in five different colours. Prepare the doughs mixing the ingredients indicated: for each one form a well in the flour, add the yeast dissolved in the water and the other ingredients. For the red and yellow doughs, first of all mix the paprika and turmeric into the flour, then continue to make the dough. For the green dough, finely blend the spinach with the water and take out just 75 g / 2 ⅔ oz of the mixture obtained, then add it to the dough.

2. Once you have prepared the five doughs, leave them to rise for about 30 minutes, then stretch them out to a thickness of one centimetre and lay various layers on top of each other, after having brushed them with beaten egg yolks [2a, 2b, 2c]. Cut strips of the dough [2d] and, with a slight twist, shape long thin rolls [2e].

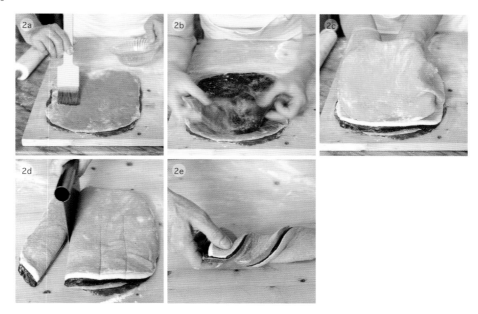

3. Wrap the long rolls in a greaseproof paper (this will ensure that the colours remain intense) and leave them to rise for around 15 minutes. Bake them in an oven preheated to 180°C / 250F for 35-40 minutes (the time will depend on the size of the rolls).

STUFFED EASTER PLAIT

- 600 g / 21 oz / 4 cups strong flour
- 370 ml / 13 fl oz / 1 ½ cups water
- 12 g brewer's yeast or 150 g / 5 ⅓ oz / 1 cup mother dough
- 30 g extra virgin olive oil
- 10 g salt
- re-milled durum wheat semolina

FOR THE DECORATION

- 5 eggs
- 20 g poppy seeds
- 20 g pumpkin seeds
- 20 g sesame seeds

FOR THE FILLING

- 100 g / 3 ½ oz / ⅔ cup crushed green olives
- 100 g / 3 ½ oz / 1 cup grated caciocavallo silano cheese
- 100 g / 3 ½ oz / 1 cup chopped soppressata salami

1. Sieve the flour and form a well in it. Dissolve the yeast in water and pour it into the flour. Start to knead, then add the salt and oil. Continue to knead the dough until you have a smooth, elastic consistency. Place it in an oiled bowl to rise and cover with a damp tea towel until it doubles in size.

2. Tip the risen dough onto the pastry board, take out a portion of about 150 g / 5 ⅓ oz and set it aside for the final decoration. Break the remaining dough into three equal parts. Shape the first piece into a long thin roll, with a rolling pin flatten it into a 8-9 cm (3 ½ in) wide strip, stuff it with crushed olives, joining the ends with your fingertips. Repeat for the two remaining pieces of dough, stuffing one with the cheese, and the other with the salami.

SOME VARIATIONS...

The ingredients for stuffing this spectacular bread may be changed as you like. Try using mushrooms cooked in olive oil, parsley and garlic, or cooked vegetables. To adapt this recipe for any occasion, you can simply omit the eggs, which are typical at Easter time.

3. Line up the three long thin rolls on a baking tray lined with greaseproof paper and sprinkled with semolina, brush with beaten egg [3a] and sprinkle each roll with a different type of seed [3b]. Plait the rolls [3c], join the ends of the plait and close it in a ring shape [3d], then stick in the remaining raw eggs in their shells, and fix them with the little strips of dough set aside previously [3e], arranging them in a cross.

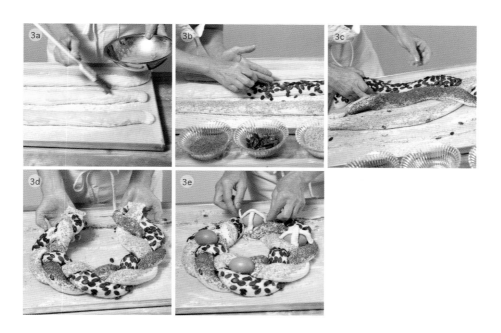

4. Leave the bread to rise for 15-20 minutes and bake in an oven preheated to 180°C / 350F for about 40-50 minutes. Serve the ring, decorating all around it, to taste, with slices of salami, lettuce leaves, shelled quails eggs and olive branches.

CHERRY TOMATO GRAPE LOAF

- 600 g / 21 ¼ oz / 4 cups strong flour
- 350 ml / 12 ⅓ fl oz / 1 ½ cups water
- 12 g brewer's yeast or 150 g / 5 ⅓ oz / 1 cup mother dough
- 10 g salt
- 20 g extra virgin olive oil

FOR THE FILLING

- basil leaves
- Pachino cherry tomatoes
- salt

TO FINISH

- a pinch of cocoa powder
- 2 or 3 spinach or basil leaves
- 10 g flour
- 2 egg yolks
- milk
- salt

1. Make a well in the sieved flour, dissolve the yeast in water and pour into the centre. Briefly knead the dough, add the salt and the oil and continue to knead until the dough is smooth and even.

2. Leave it to rise in an oiled bowl covered with a sheet of cling film or a damp cloth until the dough has doubled in size. Knock it back and take out two small pieces to form the leaves and stem of the bunch of grapes, which must then be arranged on a baking tray lined with greaseproof paper and floured. Add unsweetened cocoa powder to one piece, ideally using a mixer, and form the stem of the bunch of grapes. Blend the 10 g of flour with the spinach and add them to the second piece of dough. Use the mixture to form the leaves of the vine and a few curls.

3. With the remaining dough, form little balls, open them up with your hands to form a small disc and place a leaf of basil, a pinch of salt and a cherry tomato. If the cherry tomatoes are large, cut them in half. Close the dough around them and place each little ball face downwards on the baking tray: as you form the balls, arrange them to form a bunch. Brush the bunch with the egg yolks mixed with salt and 2 teaspoons of milk, and bake them in a preheated oven at 180°C / 350F for 35-40 minutes. This bread can work as a beautiful centrepiece.

OPEN STUFFED PLAIT

- 500 g / 17 ⅔ oz / 3 ⅓ cups strong flour
- 12 g brewer's yeast or 150 g / 5 ⅓ oz / 1 cup mother dough
- 185 ml / 6 ½ fl oz / ¾ cup milk
- 50 g sugar
- 2 large eggs
- 70 g / 2 ½ oz / ⅓ cup butter
- 7 g salt
- extra virgin olive oil

FOR THE FILLING

- 250 g / 8 ¾ oz / 1 ¼ cups dried prunes, stoned and chopped
- 120 g / 4 ¼ oz / 1 cup walnut kernels
- 4 tbsp chestnut honey
- 1 orange

1. Sieve flour, form a well in the centre and add the yeast dissolved in the milk, sugar and one egg. Combine with a fork, then add the butter at room temperature and the salt. Knead until you obtain a smooth and elastic dough. Leave to rise in an oiled bowl, covered with cling film, until it has doubled in size.

2. Meanwhile, prepare the filling: cook the prunes with a little water until they soften, drain and mash and then mix the paste, which should be quite thick, with honey, the orange rind and juice and walnut kernels.

3. Place the risen dough on a floured pastry board, spreading it out into a 50 cm (19 ½ in) long and 23 cm (9 in) wide sheet (3a, 3b).

A TIP...

You can replace the walnuts with chopped and toasted hazelnuts. The result will be even more aromatic and tasty.

4. Spread the dough with the prune filling up to 2 cm (1 in) from the edges, then roll it [4a, 4b]. Wet the edges with a drop of water to allow you to seal them properly [4c]. Leave the closing edge above the roll and, with a rolling pin, press it in the direction of the length to make the edges stick together well. Cut the dough with a sharp knife along the mark in the centre, obtaining two pieces [4d].

5. Place the two strips with the cut part uppermost and twist them around each other [5a, 5b], closing the plait at the two ends. Transfer to a baking tray lined with greaseproof paper, cover with a tea towel and leave to rise. Brush with the remaining beaten egg [5c] and bake in a preheated oven at 180°C / 350°F for about 40 minutes.

COLOURFUL PLAITS, GARLANDS AND ROLLS

FOR THE GREEN DOUGH

- 500 g / 17 ⅓ oz / 3 ⅓ cups strong flour
- 300 g / 10 ½ oz / 4 ½ cups raw spinach leaves (or chard)
- 12 g brewer's yeast or 150 g / 5 ⅓ oz / 1 cup mother dough
- 10 g honey
- 5 g salt

FOR THE WHITE DOUGH

- 500 g / 17 ⅓ oz / 2 cups strong flour
- 300 ml / 10 ½ fl oz / 1 ¼ cups water
- 12 g brewer's yeast or 150 g / 5 ⅓ oz / 1 cup mother dough
- 10 g honey
- 5 g salt

FOR THE RED DOUGH

- 500 g / 17 ⅓ oz / 2 cups strong flour
- 300 g / 10 ½ oz / 1 ½ cups tomato concentrate
- 12 g brewer's yeast or 150 g / 5 ⅓ oz / 1 cup mother dough
- 10 g honey
- 5 g salt

TO FINISH

- 1 egg
- extra virgin olive oil

1. All ingredients should be weighed in advance and be at room temperature to ensure consistent rising. You can decrease the amounts to ease preparation and cooking, or spread the work over two days.

2. To prepare the green dough, blend the spinach with 150 ml / 5 ⅓ fl oz / ⅔ cup of water until you have a smooth mixture. Take out 300g / 10 ½ oz / 4 ½ cups. Sieve the flour, add the blended spinach, the yeast dissolved in the water and the honey. Knead the ingredients, then add the salt and knead until the dough is smooth and elastic. Transfer to an oiled bowl, covered with cling film and leave to rise in a warm place until it has doubled in size. Prepare the other doughs in the same way.

3. Tip the coloured doughs onto a chopping board and shape them into the desired shapes: plaits, rolls, garlands or spirals. Leave the rolls to rise on a baking tray lined with greaseproof paper, brush with the beaten egg and bake in the oven, preheated to 200°C / 400F: it will take 15 minutes for small pieces and 20-30 minutes for the larger ones. For brighter colours, cover the baking tray with aluminium foil for the first 10 minutes of baking (in this case, it is not necessary to brush with the egg).

MEDITERRANEAN FILLED PUFF PASTRY BREAD

- 500 g / 17 ⅓ oz / 3 ⅓ cups strong flour
- 300 ml / 10 ½ fl oz / 1 ¼ cups water
- 15 g brewer's yeast or 170 g / 6 oz / 1 ¼ cups mother dough
- 200 g / 7 oz / ¾ cup butter
- 10 g salt

FOR THE FILLING

- 250 g / 8 oz / 1 ⅔ cups black and green stoned olives
- 120 g / 4 ¼ oz / ⅔ cup sun-dried tomatoes
- 50 g / oz / cups extra virgin olive oil

1. Place the sun-dried tomatoes in a bowl, cover them with water and leave them to soak for 15-20 minutes, so that they soften and lose the excess salt. Prepare a dough with all the ingredients (except the butter) and knead until it is elastic and smooth; leave it to rest in an oiled bowl for 20 minutes. In the meantime, drain the tomatoes, dry and chop finely.

2. Take the dough and roll it out with a rolling pin to form a rectangle. Dust the cold butter with a little flour and flatten it with a rolling pin. Place it on one half of the rectangle of dough, then fold the dough over the butter like a wallet, sealing the edges with your fingers. Roll out with the rolling pin, then fold the dough in three, turn it anticlockwise and roll it out again, then fold it and roll it out once more.

3. After the second turning of the pastry, form a rectangle, then scatter on the chopped olives, sun-dried tomatoes and oil. Roll the dough on itself and chop it into rounds with a thickness of about 2 cm. Arrange them on a rectangular baking tray lined with greaseproof paper, spacing them well and leave to rise until they have doubled in size. Bake in a preheated oven at 200°C / 400F for 25-30 minutes.

A SPECIAL DOUGH
This tasty recipe offers all the crumbliness of puff pastry together with the consistency and flavour of bread.

BEETROOT BREAD

- 350 g / 12 ⅓ oz / 3 cups raw beetroots
- 500 g / 17 ⅔ oz / 3 ⅓ cups strong flour
- 120 ml / 4 ⅓ fl oz / ½ cup water
- 15 g brewer's yeast or 170 g / 6 oz / 1 ¼ cup mother dough
- 40 g acacia or chestnut honey
- 4 tsp extra virgin olive oil
- 10 g salt

1. Clean the beetroots, chop into chunks and blend with the water until it has the consistency of a medium thick milkshake, sieve it and take 280 g / 9 ½ oz / 2 cups. Dissolve the yeast in two spoons of water, add the honey and combine it with the blended beetroot.

2. Sieve the flour onto a pastry board, add the beetroot mixture, salt and oil, then knead until you have a smooth, even dough. Shape it into a ball, place it in a bowl covered with a cloth and leave to rise until it has doubled in size. Tip the dough onto the pastry board, divide it into four parts and shape it into long, thin rolls. Ease them onto a baking tray lined with greaseproof paper, score the surface of the loaves and leave them to rise in a warm place until they have doubled in size.

3. Cover the loaves with a sheet of aluminium foil to maintain the brilliant colour of the beetroots, then bake them in a preheated oven at 180°C / 350F for 45-50 minutes. Take them out of the oven and leave to cool on a cooling rack.

A TIP...

To achieve a brilliant colour, it is preferable to use raw beetroots, not the precooked ones found in supermarkets.

STAR LOAF

- 500 g / 17 ⅓ oz / 3 ⅓ cups re-milled durum wheat semolina
- 100 ml / 3 ½ fl oz / ½ cup milk
- 200 ml / 7 fl oz / 1 cup water
- 12 g brewer's yeast or 150 g / 5 ⅓ oz / 1 cup mother dough
- 1 spoon of honey
- 5 g salt
- extra virgin olive oil

1. Sieve the semolina, form a well in it and pour the yeast dissolved in milk and water into the centre. Add the honey and combine with your fingertips, then add the salt. Knead until you have a soft ball of dough. Leave the dough to rise for about 30 minutes in an oiled bowl covered with a sheet of cling film.

2. Knock back the risen dough and form five oval-shaped rolls. Line a baking tray with greaseproof paper and arrange the rolls in a circle, joining them to form a star. Brush water on the parts to be joined to ensure that they remain attached after baking. Make three scores in the top of each roll with a sharp knife and leave them to rise, covered, until they double in volume.

3. Bake in a preheated oven at 220°C / 425F for 5 minutes, then reduce the temperature to 180°C / 350F and bake for about another 20 minutes.

PERFECT WITH...

This bread is excellent with red onion chutney. Clean and slice up 1.2 kg of red onions. Place them in a glass bowl, add 200 g of apple vinegar and leave to rest for two hours, covering with a cloth. Add 300 g of cane sugar, a teaspoon of salt, 3 bay leaves and the grated zest and juice of one lemon. Stir, transfer to a steal saucepan and leave to simmer over a high heat, stirring from time to time, until the chutney is thick.

SIX-ENDED PLAIT
WITH PISTACHIOS

FOR THE BIGA

- 180 g / 6 ⅓ oz / 1 ¼ cups soft wheat flour
- 125 ml / 4 ½ oz / ½ cup milk at 23°C / 73F
- 25 g brewer's yeast or 300 g / 10 ½ oz / 2 cups mother dough

FOR THE DOUGH

- 500 g / 17 ⅓ oz / 3 ⅓ cups soft wheat flour
- 70 g / 2 ½ oz / ½ cup shelled pistachios
- 50 g acacia honey
- 3 medium eggs
- 3 egg yolks
- 65 ml / 2 ¼ oz / ¼ cup extra virgin olive oil
- 15 g salt

TO FINISH

- 10 g finely chopped pistachios (optional)
- 1 egg
- extra virgin olive oil

1. Prepare the biga dissolving the yeast in the milk, add it to the flour and stir to create a smooth paste. Leave to rise in a container covered with cling film: the biga will be ready when it has doubled in volume. In the meantime, weigh the ingredients for the dough.

2. Make a well in the flour and place the honey, egg and egg yolks, oil and salt in the middle. Combine with your fingertips or a fork, then add the biga and whole pistachios. Knead until you have a smooth elastic dough. Arrange the dough in an oiled bowl that is large enough to contain the risen dough. Cover with cling film and leave to rise for about an hour or until the dough has doubled in volume.

3. Divide the dough into six equal parts and shape each one into a long, thin roll, pressing delicately with the palms of your hands. The rolls should be thicker in the middle than at the ends. Arrange them parallel to each other on the pastry board and plait the ends as explained below.

4. Join the six ends at one end and fan them out (in the photographs the rolls have been coloured to make the procedure clearer to follow). Take the last roll on the top right and cross it over to the top left [4a]. Take the roll that was the first on the left and that has now become the last but one and cross it over to the right [4b]. Separate the ends remaining at the bottom 2 by 2 [4c]. This step of separating the ends must be done at each stage. Take the top left end and cross it over to the centre, between the two pairs of ends [4d]. Take the last but one on the right and cross it over to the top left [4a]. Take the last one on the top right and cross it over to the centre [4f]. Take the last but one on the left and cross it over to the top right [4g]. Take the last one on the top right and cross it over to the centre [4h]. Take the last but one end on the right and cross it over to the top left [4i]. Take the last one on the top right and cross it over to the centre. Take the last but one end on the left and cross it over to the top right. Continue with this sequence of movements until you have used up all the dough, then close the plait, pressing the ends together well. Cut the end piece with a spatula to create a plait with a regular appearance; fold the two ends under the plait.

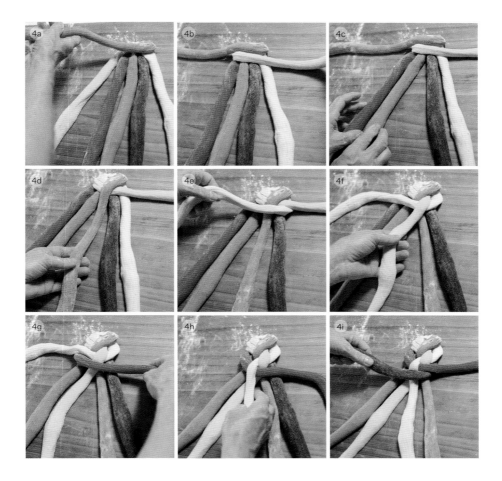

5. Place the plait on a baking tray lined with greaseproof paper in a sheltered place and leave to rise until it has doubled in volume. Preheat the oven to 180°C / 350F. Brush the dough with the beaten egg and, if you like, sprinkle the surface with chopped pistachios.

6. Place in the oven and bake for about 30 minutes: if it should brown too quickly on the top, reduce the oven temperature by about ten degrees. Remove the plait from the oven and leave it to cool completely on a cooling rack.

BREAD BASKET

- 1 kg / 35 ¼ oz / 7 cups re-milled durum wheat semolina
- 150 ml / 5 ¼ fl oz / ⅔ cup white wine vinegar
- 300 ml / 10 ½ oz / 1 ¼ cups water
- 2 eggs
- 20 g salt
- butter

1. Sieve the semolina and form a well, pour the salt dissolved in warm water into the centre, add the vinegar, combine a little flour with the liquid with a fork, then add the eggs. Knead until you have a fairly smooth and compact dough. Leave to rise for an hour wrapped in cling film.

2. If you prefer to make baskets in different colours, you can use confectioners colours, in paste or powder, to mix into the dough gradually, in order to avoid obtaining too intense a colour. You can also use liquid colourings, but in that case, you will need to take care not to make the dough too soft. If this should happen, you can remedy it by adding a little flour.

3. Roll out the dough to a thickness of about half a centimetre; with a round pastry cutter, cut out discs of 7 cm (2 ½ in) in diameter [3a], stretch them slightly with your hands, shaping them into leaves [3b], pass a grooved rolling pin for tagliolini over them [3c]

4. Place the leaves on an upside-down buttered tin of the same size that you want to make the basket. Arrange the leaves in concentric circles, starting from the bottom, placing one leaf slightly overlapping with the next [4a]. Brush them with water so that they stick together well [4b]. Press lightly on the top of the leaves so that they do not slip during baking. Continue overlapping the leaves until you have covered the entire tin [4c].

5. Bake the basket in a preheated oven at 180°C / 350F for 40-50 minutes. Leave in the basket in the oven until it has dried out. Take it out of the tin carefully and when it is completely cool and dry, keep it in a cloth or plastic bag.

LET YOUR CREATIVITY FLOW...

With the same technique, you can make baskets of different sizes, using small or large tins depending on the amount of bread that you want to fit into it. You can also get creative with the shapes, using oval, rectangular or contoured tins, or creating a plaited cover on a simple round tin. All you need is a bit of practice and lots of imagination!

CHEESE RING

- 700 g / 24 ¾ oz / 4 ⅔ cups strong flour
- 250 g / 8 ¾ oz / 2 ½ cups mild pecorino cheese
- 25 g brewer's yeast or 300 g / 10 ⅔ oz / 2 cups mother dough
- 335 ml / 11 ¾ oz / 1 ⅓ cups milk
- 1 medium egg
- 120 g / 4 ¼ oz / ½ cup butter
- 1 tbsp malt (or honey)
- 1 tbsp fennel seeds
- 10 g salt
- 1 egg yolk
- peppercorns
- extra virgin olive oil
- milk

1. Sieve the flour, make a well in the centre and pour in the yeast dissolved in warm milk. Add the whole egg, slightly beaten, the malt and the soft butter. Combine with your finger tips or with a fork and add the salt. Knead the ingredients until you have a smooth and elastic dough. Form it into a ball, transfer it to a bowl brushed with oil, cover with cling film and leave to rise for an hour in a warm place.

2. Knock back the dough and combine the pecorino in cubes, a grinding of pepper and the fennel seeds. Divide it into three long thin rolls, plait them and transfer the plait to a 28 cm (11 in) diameter tin lined with greaseproof paper; join the ends to make a ring, brush the surface with the egg yolk, lightly salted and diluted with a spoonful of milk. Leave the ring to rise for about 30 minutes and bake it in a preheated oven at 190 °C / 375F for 40-45 minutes.

A TIP...

As an alternative to the pecorino, you could also use another kind of cheese, such as groviera, caciocavallo or fontina.

MINI PANETTONES WITH PEANUT GLAZE

- 500 g / 17 ⅔ oz / 2 cups strong flour
- 150 g / 5 ¼ oz / 1 ½ cups salted peanuts
- 250 g / 8 ¾ oz / 1 ⅔ cups mother dough
- 240 ml / 8 ½ fl oz / 1 cup whole milk
- 20 g brewer's yeast
- 1 egg
- 2 egg yolks
- 50 g sugar
- 75 g / 2 ⅔ oz / ⅓ cup butter
- 5 g salt

FOR THE GLAZE

- 50 g peanuts
- 2 egg whites
- 25 g grain

1. In a bowl, dissolve the mother dough with the milk, add the brewer's yeast, egg and egg yolks. Form a well in the flour and peanuts and add the mixture you have just prepared, then knead until you have a smooth and elastic dough. Halfway through kneading, add the salt, sugar and softened butter; continue to knead for at least 10 minutes.

2. Leave the dough to rise for 20 minutes. Break it up into little balls each weighing 50 g, place in little tins, similar to those used for panettone and leave to rise until they have doubled in volume.

3. Prepare the glaze by combining the blended peanuts, egg whites and grain, then spread it over the surface of the panettones with a pastry bag with a flat nozzle. Bake the panettones in the oven at 220°C / 425F for 15-20 minutes.

A TIP...

You can also prepare these delicious appetisers by cooking them on a baking tray covered with greaseproof paper, without putting them in the panettone tins. You will end up with some tasty rolls!

PLAITED ROLLS WITH CURRANTS

- 500 g / 17 ⅔ oz / 2 cups strong flour
- 265 ml / 9 ⅓ fl oz / 1 cup milk
- 70 g / 2 ½ oz / ⅓ cup currants
- 15 g brewer's yeast or 150 g / 5 ⅓ oz / 1 cup mother dough
- 1 medium egg
- 2 tbsp honey
- 50 g / 1 ¾ oz / ¼ cup butter
- 10 g salt
- 1 egg yolk
- milk

1. Sieve the flour, add the yeast dissolved in milk and begin to knead the ingredients. Halfway through kneading, add the salt, egg and last of all, the honey and butter. Leave to rest for about 15 minutes, then add the currants and mix into the dough.

2. Break the dough into two equal parts. With one part, form little balls and the other little plaits. Arrange the rolls and plaits on baking trays and brush with the egg yolk, lightly salted and diluted in two teaspoons of milk. Leave them to rise until they have doubled in volume at a temperature of about 27 °C / 80F.

3. Brush them with egg yolk again and bake for 8-10 minutes in a preheated oven at 200-210°C / 400-415F, placing 5-6 ice cubes on the bottom of the oven to make steam. The baking time depends on the size of the pieces. 10 minutes will be enough for rolls weighing 30 g.

CURRANTS

By contrast to normal raisins, currants are small, round, dark and seedless. Generally speaking they are imported from the Middle East and can be found in specialty food shops. If you cannot get currants, you can use ordinary raisins, cutting them in half.

LIMONCINI

- 500 g / 17 ⅔ oz / 3 ⅓ cups strong flour
- 60 ml / 2 fl oz / ¼ cup lemon juice
- zest of 1 ½ lemons
- 15 g brewer's yeast
- 250 ml / 8 ¾ fl oz / 1 cup water
- 150 g / 5 ⅓ oz / 1 cup mother dough
- 10 g salt

TO FINISH

- 1 egg
- 15 g milk
- salt

1. Dissolve the brewer's yeast in the warm water. Add the mother dough, sieved flour, and salt and knead for 4-5 minutes, then add the lemon juice and grated zest and combine all the ingredients. Leave to rest for 45 minutes in a very warm place.

2. Break the dough into portions, each weighing 50-60 g. Shape them into ovals, then press lightly on the ends of the rolls and roll them over a cheese grater to give them the appearance of a lemon. Make them shiny by brushing them with the egg mixed with the milk and a pinch of salt.

3. Leave the limoncini to rise for about an hour in a warm place and bake them in a preheated oven at 220°C / 425F with the steam of 4-5 ice cubes placed on the bottom of the oven. They will take about 20 minutes to bake.

PERFECT WITH...

These rolls are excellent with lemon marmalade. Scrape the zest of 1 kg of lemons with a fork and leave them to soak in cold water for 24 hours, changing the water several times; slice them and simmer them in a steel saucepan with an inch of water, stirring until all the liquid has dried up. In a separate saucepan, simmer 600 g of sugar with 250 g of water until you have a syrup. Add it to the lemons and simmer, stirring, for another 15 minutes.

CHOCOLATE AND RAISIN BAGUETTE

- 600 g / 21 oz / 4 cups strong flour
- 20 g / ¾ oz / 5 tsp cocoa
- 100 g / 3 ½ oz / ½ cup raisins
- 12 g brewer's yeast or 150 g / 5 ⅓ oz / ¾ cup mother dough
- 350 ml / 12 ⅓ fl oz / 1 ½ cups water
- 30 g / 1 oz / 2 tbsp butter
- 10 g salt
- extra virgin olive oil

1. Sieve the flour with the cocoa, form a well and pour the yeast dissolved in the water at 22-23°C. Combine the ingredients and then add the salt, softened butter and raisins. Knead the dough until it is fairly soft and smooth. Leave the dough to rest for about 15 minutes in oiled bowl and covered in a sheet of cling film.

2. Turn the dough out onto a floured surface and form the baguettes to the size you want. Score the surface diagonally and leave them to rise for about 30 minutes. Bake the baguette in a preheated oven at 200°C / 400F. 20 minutes is sufficient for small pieces, whereas larger loaves will need 25 minutes more.

PERFECT WITH...

Despite containing cocoa, this is not a sweet bread and it can be eaten with jam or hazelnut chocolate spread, or with savoury, meat-based products.

BREAD WITH OLIVES AND CHEESE

- 300 g / 10 ½ oz / 2 cups strong flour
- 100 g / 3 ½ oz / ⅔ cup stoned green olives
- 25 g black olive paste
- 100 g / 3 ½ oz / 1 cup grated provolone silano cheese
- 12 g brewer's yeast or 150 g / 5 ⅓ oz / 1 cup mother dough
- 145 ml / 5 fl oz / ⅔ cup milk
- 3 eggs
- 30 g extra virgin olive oil
- 5 g salt
- butter

1. Dissolve the yeast in warm milk (22-23°C / 71-73F), add the beaten eggs, mix the liquids and then incorporate the sieved flour. Knead the dough vigorously with your hands until the dough is quite soft but has no lumps. Add the salt and oil and continue to knead for a few minutes.

2. Add the olives chopped into rounds, the grated cheese and finally the black olive paste. Transfer the dough into a greased and floured 28 cm (11 in) loaf tin, filling it ¾ to full, cover with a sheet of cling film and leave the bread to rise, away from any drafts, until it doubles in volume. Bake in the oven at 180°C / 350F for 40-45 minutes.

PERFECT WITH...

This substantial, tasty bread can work as a standalone dish, but it is also perfect with cured meats or vegetable frittatas.

AROMATIC HERB ROLL

- 250 g / 8 ¾ oz / 1 ⅔ cups strong flour
- 250 g / 8 ¾ oz / 1 ⅔ cups soft wheat flour
- 12 g brewer's yeast or 100 g / 3 ½ oz / ⅔ cup mother dough
- 190 ml / 6 ⅔ fl oz / ¾ cup milk
- 50 ml / 2 fl oz / ½ cup melted butter
- 1 large egg
- 1 tsp honey
- ½ tsp salt

FOR THE FILLING

- 1 clove of garlic
- 1 egg yolk
- 100 g / 3 ½ oz / 1 cup mixed herbs (parsley, chives, basil and a few spinach leaves)
- a pinch of oregano
- 70 g / 2 ½ oz / ⅔ cup chopped nuts (hazelnuts, almond, walnuts, pistachios)
- 100 g / 3 ½ oz / ⅔ cup stoned green olives
- 30 g extra virgin olive oil
- salt

TO FINISH

- butter
- 1 small cup of coffee

1. Mix and sieve the flours, form a well in the centre and pour in the yeast dissolved in the warm milk, the melted (but not hot) butter, the egg and the honey. Mix and add the salt. Knead until the dough is soft and smooth. Place the dough in an oiled bowl and leave to rise until it doubles in volume. In the meantime, mash the garlic until it is mushy. Place it in a bowl with the oil and egg yolk and combine.

2. Take the risen dough, stretch it into an elongated rectangle with your hands and brush the dough with the garlic mash. Combine the chopped chives, parsley, basil, spinach, oregano, nuts and chopped olives, spread the mixture over the surface, setting aside 2 spoonfuls.

3. Roll the dough from both short sides until they reach the middle. Before bringing the two rolled sides together, spread the stuffing set aside between them, close and place the roll in a greased and floured 28 cm (11 in) loaf tin. Leave to rise for about 45 minutes, then brush the surface with the coffee: This will ensure that the roll has a warm brown colour, without taking on particular aromas. Bake in a preheated oven at 180°C / 350F for 45-50 minutes.

STUFFED FRIED BREAD BALLS

- 500 g / 17 ⅔ oz / 3 ⅓ cups strong flour
- 500 g / 18 oz / 2 ¼ cups potatoes
- 2 eggs
- 12 g brewer's yeast
- 2 tbsp extra virgin olive oil
- 5 g salt
- peanut oil for frying

FOR THE FILLING

- 2 smoked scamorza cheeses
- 200 g / 7 oz / 1 ⅓ cups mortadella

1. Boil the potatoes whole, skins on, strain, mash and add them to the flour while they are still warm. Dissolve the yeast in a little water, add it to the potato and flour mixture, add the eggs and oil and knead for 3-4 minutes, add the salt and knead for another minute.

2. Finely chop the cheese with the mortadella. Spread out the dough and with a pastry cutter, cut out discs of 3-4 cm (1 ½ in) in diameter, stuff them with the chopped cheese and mortadella and close them to form little balls with your hands. Leave to rise until they have doubled in volume and fry them in plenty of hot oil.

A TIP...

If you want a lesser quantity of bread balls, you can half the amounts of ingredients. It is also possible to freeze some of them, then heat them up in the oven before use.

FIG AND POPPY SEED BUTTER BREAD

- 400 g / 14 oz / 2 ⅔ cups soft wheat flour
- 10 g brewer's yeast or 100 g / 3 ½ oz / ½ cup mother dough
- 95 ml / 3 ⅓ fl oz / ⅓ cup milk
- 1 tsp honey
- 3 eggs
- 80 g / 2 ¾ oz / ⅓ cup butter
- 5 g salt
- 1 egg yolk
- extra virgin olive oil

FOR THE FILLING

- 120 g / 4 ¼ oz / 1 cup poppy seeds
- 250 g / 8 ¾ oz / 1 ½ cups dried figs
- 3 tbsp orange
- blossom honey
- zest of 1 orange
- 85 ml / 3 oz / ⅓ cup di Passito di Pantelleria raisin wine

1. Prepare the dough: Dissolve the yeast in the warm milk and 130 g of flour, make a soft dough and leave to rise covered with a cloth for about 30 minutes. Meanwhile, put the figs cut into small pieces to soften in the raisin wine, so that they absorb completely.

2. Put the poppy seeds in a bowl, cover with boiling water and let them rest for 5 minutes, then drain, transfer them to a saucepan, add honey, bring to a boil and simmer for 5 minutes. Remove from heat and let cool. Combine the cooled seeds, figs, raisin wine and orange rind, mix well.

3. Form a well with the remaining flour. In the middle, put the eggs, honey, softened butter and salt; add the prepared dough. Knead until the mixture is consistent and smooth. If the mixture is dry, add a little milk; if it sticks to the fingers, add a little flour. Place the dough in a greased bowl of oil, cover with plastic wrap and let rise until doubled in volume.

4. Turn out the risen dough onto a floured surface and spread out to form a rectangle. Spread the filling all over the dough, roll it up and brush the join with water to seal it well. Place the roll on a baking tray lined with greaseproof paper, with the join facing downwards and leave to rise for 15 minutes. Brush with the egg yolk, lightly salted diluted with a drop of milk. Bake in a preheated oven at 180°C / 350F for 30-35 minutes.

SEMOLINA FRUSTINE WITH BAKED OLIVES

- 600 g / 21 oz / 4 cups re-milled durum wheat semolina
- 12 g brewer's yeast or 150 g / 5 ⅓ oz / 1 cup mother dough
- 350 ml / 12 ⅓ fl oz / 1 ½ cups water
- 55 ml / 2 oz / ¼ cup extra virgin olive oil
- 10 g salt (1 teaspoon)

FOR THE FILLING

- 200 g / 7 oz / 1 ⅓ cups stoned black olives
- 160 ml / 5 ⅔ oz / ⅔ cup extra virgin olive oil
- 3 cloves of garlic
- 3 sprigs of rosemary
- oregano
- 1 tsp 'nduja (optional)

1. Dissolve the yeast with the water, add it to the sieved flour and knead slightly. Add the salt and oil and knead the dough until it is smooth. Tip the dough into an oiled bowl, covered with a damp cloth and leave to rise in a warm place until it has doubled in volume.

2. In a small saucepan over a low heat, gently fry the garlic in its skin and put rosemary in the oil, taking care that it doesn't burn. Leave it to brown only as long as necessary to extract the essential oils. Take out the garlic and rosemary, add the finely chopped olives and leave them to take on the flavours for a few minutes. Remove from the heat and leave to cool.

A TIP...

Frustine stay crispy for several days. If you want them to keep for longer, after baking you can leave them to dry in the oven at 160°C for another 15 minutes.

3. Turn the dough out onto a (non-wooden) surface dusted with semolina, knock it back and form a rectangle of about 35 x 70 cm (13 x 27 in), and a thickness of half a centimetre. Pour over the oil with the olives and spread it evenly all over with your hands [3a], then sprinkle with oregano and complete to taste with lumps of 'nduja. With a pizza cutter, cut one-centimetre-wide strips out of the short side of the dough [3b]. Fold each strip over on itself, pressing to make the two touching surfaces stick well [3c], then twist it to create the typical frusta shape [3d].

4. Gently lay the frustine on a baking tray lined with greaseproof paper and bake them in a preheated oven at 200°C / 400F for about 15-20 minutes, or until they are golden brown. Take them out of the oven and leave to cool.

WHOLE GRAIN CROSTINI WITH FENNEL SEEDS

- 700 g / 24 ⅔ oz / 4 ⅔ cups whole grain flour
- fennel seeds
- 15 g brewer's yeast or 200 g / 7 oz / 1 ⅓ cups mother dough
- 350 ml / 12 ⅓ fl oz / 1 ½ cups water
- 75 ml / ¼ fl oz / ⅓ cup extra virgin olive oil
- 12 g salt

1. Pour the flour on a work surface, forming a well in the middle. Add the yeast, dissolved in water, combine part of the flour and then add the oil and salt. Knead the mixture until smooth and elastic. Let the dough rise in an oiled bowl covered with cling film until double in volume.

2. Knock back the risen dough and form large sticks with a diameter of about 3 cm (1 in). Spread a chopping board with fennel seeds and roll the sticks of dough in them to cover.

3. Cut again into squares of around 3 cm (1 in). Place them on a baking tin lined with baking paper, let them rise for 15 minutes and cook in an oven, preheated to 180°C / 350F for 20 minutes. Reduce to 150°C / 300F and cook for another 20 minutes. These crostini will keep for several days wrapped in cling film or kept in a sandwich bag. You could also make this recipe by dividing the dough into two equal parts and flavouring some with fennel seeds and the other with chilli or other seeds to your taste.

CRISPY BREAD TONGUES

- 250 g / 8 ¾ oz / 1 ⅔ cups re-milled durum wheat semolina
- 150 g / 5 ⅓ oz / 1 cup fine milled maize flour (Fioretto)
- 12 g brewer's yeast
- 230 ml / 8 fl oz / 1 cup water
- 85 ml / 3 fl oz / ⅓ cup extra virgin olive oil
- 5 g salt

1. Dissolve the yeast in the water at 22-23°C / 71-73F. Place the sieved semolina and flour on a pastry board, make a well in the centre, pour in the dissolved yeast and knead. Add the salt and oil and continue to knead until it is smooth and compact. Transfer the dough to a large oiled bowl, cover with a damp cloth, place it away from any draughts and leave it to rise until it has doubled in volume.

2. Transfer the dough to a pastry board, stretch it out with your hands to form a rectangle with a thickness of one centimetre. Cut 2 cm (1 in) wide strips with a pizza cutter and then cut the strips into 3 cm (1 in) pieces. Flour and pass one by one into a pasta machine, first at a medium thickness and then at the last level but one. You should get 'tongues' that are fine but not too fragile (with a similar thickness to the traditional Sardinian flat bread, pane carasau).

3. Dust the tongues on both sides with the semolina and place them on a rectangular baking tray lined with greaseproof paper. Bake them in a preheated oven at the maximum temperature for a few minutes until they are turning golden brown, turning them over halfway through the baking time if necessary.

PERFECT WITH...

These crunchy tongues are excellent with a tomato and ginger chutney. Wash 1 kg of tomatoes, plunge them into boiling water, then remove their skins and seeds. Chop into pieces and place in a saucepan with the juice and grated zest of one lemon, 15 g of grated ginger and a teaspoon of salt. Leave to simmer for 20 minutes, stirring. Prepare a syrup by placing 70 g of water and 300 g of sugar over a low heat. When the tomatoes have dried up the liquid, add the syrup and simmer for 5 minutes. The chutney is ready when a drop poured onto a tilted plate does not slide away but congeals rapidly.

GRISSINI

- 600 g / 21 oz / 4 cups strong flour
- 15 g brewer's yeast or 150 g / 5 ⅓ oz / 1 cup mother dough
- 250 ml / 8 ¾ oz / 1 cup water
- 110 ml / 4 fl oz / ½ cup extra virgin olive oil (or 60 g lard)
- 10 g salt
- 2 eggs
- sesame, poppy and sunflower seeds

1. Sieve the flour. Dissolve the yeast in the water, add the flour and knead. In this initial phase, given that the dough is very hard, it is a good idea to use a mixer. After a few minutes, add the salt and the oil and continue to knead until the dough is smooth and even.

2. Place the dough in an oiled container, cover with a sheet of cling film and leave to rise until it has doubled in volume. Stretch it out with your hands until it has a thickness of one centimetre. With a pizza cutter, cut 1 cm wide strips of the desired length.

3. In a dish, beat the eggs with a fork. Spread out the various seeds on sheets of aluminium foil. Take one strip of dough at a time. Holding the strip at the end with your fingers, first dip it in the egg and then the seeds. Gently place the strips on a rectangular baking tray lined with greaseproof paper and leave them to rise for about another 15 minutes. Bake in a preheated oven at 200°C / 400F for 20 minutes, then reduce the temperature to 150°C / 300F and leave to bake for a further 15 minutes.

OLIVE OIL TARALLUCCI

- 500 g / 17 ⅔ oz / 2 cups strong flour
- 110 ml / 4 oz / ½ cup extra virgin olive oil
- 1 egg
- 12 g brewer's yeast or 150 g / 5 ¼ oz / 1 cup mother dough
- 150 ml / 5 ¼ oz / ⅔ cup dry white wine
- 7 g salt
- 30 g fennel seeds

1. Sift flour and form a well, put the egg and the yeast, dissolved in a tablespoon of water, in the middle and combine, add wine, oil, salt and fennel seeds. Knead until smooth and elastic. Place the dough in an oil-greased bowl, cover with a sheet of cling film and let it rise in a warm place for 30 minutes

2. Form the dough into a long sausage. Cut one centimetre thick rounds and roll them on the pastry board lots of little sausages of the size of a finger, then close them to form lots of little rings and seal them well by squashing them with your fingers at the ends to avoid them opening while cooking. As you have them ready, arrange the rings on a cloth. Cover with another cloth and leave to rise for 30 minutes.

3. Cook the tarallucci in salted boiling water and take them out with a slotted spoon as they rise to the top. Boiling them is what makes the surfaces shiny. Leave them to drain on a cotton cloth overnight; this step of leaving them to rest is not compulsory but improves the final result. Arrange them on a baking tray lined with greaseproof paper and bake them in a preheated oven at 200°C / 400F for about 20 minutes or until they start to turn golden.

A TIP...

You can create tasty variations by adding chilli powder, oregano or finely chopped olives to the dough.

BRIOCHE WITH CHEESE, PROSCIUTTO AND PEAS

- 500 g / 17 ⅔ oz / 3 ⅓ cups strong flour
- 12 g brewer's yeast or 150 g / 5 ⅓ oz / 1 cup mother dough
- 125 ml / 4 ⅓ fl oz / ½ cup milk
- 3 large eggs
- 1 tbsp acacia honey
- 30 ml / 2 tbsp extra virgin olive oil
- 5 g salt (1 tsp)

FOR THE FILLING

- 250 g / 8 ¾ oz / 2 ½ cups caciocavallo silano cheese
- 100 g / 3 ½ oz / ⅔ cup thin sliced prosciutto
- 200 g / 7 oz / 1 ⅓ cups fresh podded peas
- 1 clove of garlic
- 325 ml / 11 ½ oz / 1 ⅓ cups bechamel sauce
- 1 egg yolk
- 50 g butter
- salt

TO FINISH

- 1 egg yolk
- milk
- salt

1. Sieve the flour onto the pastry board, make a well in the centre and pour in the yeast dissolved in the warm milk, eggs, honey and oil. Combine and add the salt. Knead the dough, which must be soft. Form it into a ball and leave to rest, covered with a tea towel, for about an hour.

2. For the filling, cook the peas in a frying pan with the garlic and butter for about 12 minutes, gradually adding a little water if necessary. Adjust the salt to taste, remove from the heat and leave to cool. Roughly chop the cheese.

3. Roll out ⅔ of the dough and line a greased and floured cake tin with a diameter of 24 cm (9 ½ in) and a height of 4 cm (1 ½ in). Place the slices of prosciutto half of the peas and the bechamel, with the egg yolk, chopped cheese and remaining peas already added, on top of the dough base.

4. Brush the edges with the egg yolk, lightly salted and mixed with two teaspoons of milk, and close the brioche with the second sheet. Leave to rise in a warm place for about an hour. Brush all over the surface with the remaining egg yolk and bake in a preheated oven at 180°C / 350F for about 40 minutes.

SERRESE PITTA WITH ELDERFLOWERS

- 400 g / 14 oz / 2 ⅔ cups strong flour
- 12 g brewer's yeast or 150 g / 5 ⅓ oz / 1 cup mother dough
- 220 ml / 7 ¾ oz / 1 cup water
- 30 ml extra virgin olive oil
- 5 g salt

FOR THE FILLING

- 1 tsp dried elderflowers
- 300 g / 10 ½ oz / 2 cups green olives
- 350 g / 12 ⅓ oz / 2 ⅓ cups red Tropea spring onions with the green stems (or red Tropea onions)
- 4 or 5 anchovy fillets
- 30 ml extra virgin olive oil
- salt

1. Sieve the flour into a bowl and make a well in the centre. Pour in the yeast, diluted with water, mix with part of the flour, then add the oil and salt. Knead all of the ingredients until the dough is firm and elastic. Form a ball, place it in an oiled bowl, cover with a damp cloth and leave to rise in a warm place until it doubles in volume.

2. For the filling, clean and wash the spring onions, eliminating the outer layer. Chop into slices and cut the green parts into little pieces. Wilt for 4-5 minutes in a frying pan with the olive oil and a pinch of salt. Remove from the heat and leave to cool. Add the anchovy fillets and mix well. Stone the olives, finely chop, add them to the cooled onions and flavour with the elderflowers.

3. With a rolling pin, roll out the dough into a rectangular-shaped fine sheet. Spread the mixture over half of the sheet leaving the edges free. Close the pitta like a book and seal the outer edges. Place it on a baking tray lined with floured greaseproof paper and leave to rise for 15-20 minutes. Brush the surface with oil and bake in a preheated oven at 180°C / 350F for about 40 minutes.

ELDERFLOWERS

The umbrella-shaped flowers of this bush are picked from May to July and are left to dry in the shade. They can be used against colds and flu or as a mask for swollen eyes and have many more medicinal properties. They can also be found at herbalist shops.

APPLE AND CINNAMON PIZZA

- 1 kg / 35 ¼ oz / 7 cups pizza dough
- 3 large apples
- 1 tsp ground cinnamon
- 1 unwaxed lemon
- 70 g / 2 ½ oz / ⅓ cup raw cane sugar
- 70 g / 2 ½ oz / ⅓ cup butter
- re-milled durum wheat semolina (for dusting)

1. Prepare the pizza dough according to the basic recipe. While the dough is rising, peel the apples, finely slice, place in a large bowl and season with the juice of half a lemon, all of the grated zest, half a teaspoon of cinnamon and 40 g of cane sugar. Leave the flavours to develop until the dough has risen.

2. Line a rectangular tin with greaseproof paper, dust with durum wheat semolina and stretch out the dough with your fingers to a thickness of half a centimetre (or the desired height). Spread the apples over the top of the dough and finish by spreading with the remaining cane sugar and remaining cinnamon. Scatter knobs of butter over the top to finish.

3. Bake the pizza in a preheated oven at 220-240°C / 425-475F, placing the baking tray in the bottom part of the oven for 10 minutes and then moving it to mid height for another 20-25 minutes or until the pizza is done. Remove from the oven and leave to cool a little before serving.

A SWEET PIZZA

Pizza dough is ideal used with sweet toppings. This recipe is one example, in which the contrast between the savoury base and the sweet topping creates a particularly tasty combination.

COURGETTE AND STRACCHINO PIZZA

- 1 kg / 35 ¼ oz / 7 cups pizza dough
- 4-5 romanesco courgettes
- 200 g / 7 oz / 2 cups stracchino cheese
- 1 tsp oregano
- extra virgin olive oil
- 5 g salt
- re-milled durum wheat semolina

1. Prepare the pizza dough according to the basic recipe. While the dough is rising, leave the courgettes to soak, sliced into fine rounds using a mandoline, with 55 ml olive oil, salt and oregano. Leave to rest for about an hour then throw away the vegetable water.

2. Line a rectangular tin with greaseproof paper, dust with durum wheat semolina and stretch out the dough, to a thickness of half a centimetre. Bake the pizza in a preheated oven at 220°C / 425F, placing the baking tray in the bottom part of the oven for 10 minutes and then moving it to the middle of the oven for another 10 minutes.

3. Remove the pizza from the oven, cover it with the courgette rounds, another sprinkling of oregano, a drizzle of oil and the blobs of stracchino. Place back in the middle of the oven and finish cooking. It will take about 10 minutes.

A TIP...

A few more tasty ideas for pizza toppings: julienned radicchio and smoked provola cheese, sliced artichokes and robiola cheese, porcini cooked with olive oil, parsley and garlic and mozzarella.

PIZZA, FIGS AND MORTADELLA

- 750 g / 26 ½ oz / 5 cups strong flour
- 20 g brewer's yeast or 7 g dried yeast
- 415 ml / 14 ⅔ oz / 1 ¾ cups water
- 10 g malt or honey
- 50 g extra virgin olive oil
- 15 g salt

FOR THE BRINE

- 50 ml / 1 ¾ oz / 3 ½ tbsp water
- 50 ml olive oil
- 10 g salt

FOR THE FILLING

- 1 kg / 35 oz / 6 cups ripe figs
- 150 g / 5 ⅓ oz / 1 cup mortadella

1. Sieve the flour, make a well in the centre and pour the yeast dissolved in the water at 22-23°C / 71-73F and the malt into it. Knead the ingredients. Halfway through kneading add the oil and salt; knead until smooth. Place the dough in an oiled bowl, cover with a cloth and leave to rise for about an hour. Alternatively, you can knead the same quantities of ingredients with 5 g of brewer's yeast or 100 g of mother dough. Then place the dough back in an oiled bowl, cover with cling film and leave to rise in the fridge for 24 hours. Leave the dough at room temperature for an hour before using it.

2. At the end of this time, tip the dough onto the pastry board and stretch it out with your hands. Transfer to a rectangular baking tray, giving the dough the desired thickness (thicker for soft pizza, thinner for crispy) and leave to rise for 30 minutes.

3. Prepare the brine: dissolve the salt in the hot water and add the oil, beating well with a whisk to make an emulsion. Spread half of the brine evenly over the spread out dough, then make some deep holes with your fingers and place in the oven at 240°C / 475F for 20 minutes.

4. Remove the pizza from the oven and spread in the remaining emulsion. Bake in a hot over for 10 minutes or until golden. Allow to cool and fill with mortadella and halved figs.

FILO QUICHE WITH TUNA AND CHICORY

FOR THE FILO PASTRY

- 250 g / 8 ¾ oz / 1 ⅔ cups strong flour
- 150 ml / 5 ⅓ fl oz / ⅔ cup water
- extra virgin olive oil

FOR THE FILLING

- 260 g / 9 oz / 1 ⅔ cups tuna fillets in oil
- 400 g / 14 oz / 3 cups chicory (endives)
- 1 clove of garlic
- 3 eggs
- 145 ml / 5 oz / ⅔ cup milk
- ½ tsp oregano
- 150 g / 5 ⅓ oz / 1 ½ cups primo sale pecorino (or provola) cheese
- 200 g / 7 oz / 1 ⅓ cups cherry tomatoes
- 30 g extra virgin olive oil
- salt

1. Sieve the flour onto the pastry board, make a well in the centre. Knead with the water until the dough is soft and smooth. Form it into a ball, cover with a damp cloth and leave to rest for 15 minutes. Roll the dough into a sausage shape and divide it into nine equal parts, rolling them into little balls. Cover with a damp cloth so that the dough does not dry out.

2. Roll out the first three balls with a rolling pin to obtain three discs with a thickness of just a few millimetres. Continue to make the filo pastry: you will need three sheets.

3. For the filling, chop the chicory into large pieces, place in a saucepan with the oil and garlic in its skin and stew with the lid on for 4-5 minutes. Remove the garlic and leave to cool. In a bowl, beat the eggs, add the milk, oregano, roughly crumbled tuna fillets, cheese, in pieces and cooled chicory. Add salt to taste.

4. Line a 5 cm (2 in) deep baking tin with a diameter of 24 cm (9 ½ in) with greaseproof paper, gently place the first sheet of pastry inside so that it reaches 3 cm (1 ¼ in) above the top of the tin and brush with oil, do the same with the other two sheets. Spread the filling on the pastry base, close the edges over each other and brush with oil. Bake in a preheated oven at 220°C / 425F for 10 minutes, then reduce the temperature to 180°C / 350F and bake for a further 25-30 minutes.

HERB AND SOFT CHEESE FILO TRIANGLES

FOR THE FILO PASTRY

- 250 g / 8 ¾ oz / 1 ⅔ cups strong flour
- 150 ml / 5 ⅓ oz / ⅔ cup water
- extra virgin olive oil

FOR THE FILLING

- 200 g / 7 oz / 2 cups chard
- 100 g / 3 ½ oz / 1 cup stracchino cheese
- 1 spring onion
- 8 walnut kernels
- 10 black olives
- 1 tbsp raisins
- 1 sprig of parsley
- a few sprigs of marjoram
- hot chilli powder
- extra virgin olive oil
- salt

1. For the filling, remove the hard part of the chard stalks and chop the rest into strips. Finely chop the spring onion, crush the walnuts, stone and finely chop the olives and put the raisins in warm water to soak. Brown the onion in a drop of oil, add the chard, cover and leave to simmer for 5 minutes. Remove the cover, salt and allow the remaining water to evaporate. Leave to cool and add the strained raisins, walnuts, chilli, stracchino cheese, olives and finely chopped herbs.

2. Prepare the filo pastry with the ingredients indicated, following the steps described previously. Cut out long strips from the filo pastry, dip them in a drop of oil and place a spoonful of filling on one end.

3. Fold the corner of the strip over the filling, so that it covers it with a pastry triangle [3a,]. Fold the pastry again, bringing the edge of the triangle to the top and continue like this until the end of the strip [3b, 3c]. You will end up with a triangle over which you will fold the last strip of pastry [3d].

4. Brush the triangles with oil on both sides and bake in a preheated oven at 180°C / 350F for 15-20 minutes or until they are crispy and golden. In the Balkans, these triangles are stuffed with various fillings and are known as börek.

A TIP...

Filo pastry triangles can also be made with other fillings. Try them with sausage and broccoli or ham and emmental.

BAKLAVA

- 500 g / 17 ⅔ oz / 3 ⅓ cups soft wheat flour
- about 250 ml / 8 ¾ oz / 1 cup water
- 2 egg yolks
- potato starch (or corn starch)
- salt
- corn seed oil

FOR THE FILLING

- 200 g / 7 oz / 1 ⅔ cups chopped hazelnuts (cob nuts)
- 200 g / 7 oz / 1 ⅔ cups shelled unsalted pistachios (or other nut, to taste)

FOR THE SYRUP

- 500 g / 17 ⅔ oz / 2 ¼ cups sugar
- 300 ml / 10 ½ oz / 1 ¼ cups water
- 2 cinnamon sticks
- 3 cloves

FOR BRUSHING

- 200 g / 7 oz / ¾ cup butter

1. Sieve the flour onto a pastry board, make a well in the centre and knead with the water, egg yolks and a pinch of salt, working until you have a soft, smooth dough. Form it into a ball, cover with a damp cloth and leave to rest for about 30 minutes. Divide the pastry into lots of little balls of the same weight (the total number must be a multiple of 5) and roll them out one at a time with a rolling pin, so you end up with lots of little discs with a thickness of a few millimetres. When rolling out the discs, flour the work surface and pastry discs with potato starch or corn starch only.

2. Prepare the sheets of pastry using 5 discs of dough, brushing each layer with excellent quality corn seed oil and overlaying them, avoiding oiling the top surface. Lay out the sheets of pastry on cloths. Gently place a sheet of pastry in a greased 5 cm (2 in) deep, 30 x 40 cm (12 x 16 in) baking tin, allowing it to hang over the edges. Brush with melted butter and overlay another two sheets of pastry: between one sheet of pastry and the next brush with more butter. Trim the edges of the pastry and, reusing the pieces, make more sheets of pastry (join them up like a collage without mixing them again).

3. Form a layer of pistachios. Cover with three sheets of pastry, form a layer of walnuts and cover with another three sheets of pastry. Cut deeply into the baklava with an oiled knife to create diamond shapes. Pour the remaining melted butter on the top and into the incisions. Bake in a preheated oven at 180°C / 350F for an hour or until the cuts start to open.

4. Bring water, sugar, cinnamon and cloves to a temperature of about 110°C / 230F or leave to simmer until the mixture has taken on a sugary consistency. Drizzle the baklava with the syrup and leave to rest for 12 hours.

FILO CANNOLI WITH RICOTTA AND PISTACHIOS

FOR THE FILO PASTRY

- 150 g / 5 ⅓ oz / 1 cup flour
- 80 ml / 2 ¾ oz / ⅓ cup water
- a pinch of salt

FOR THE FILLING

- 500 g / 17 ⅔ oz / 5 cups sheep's milk ricotta
- 30 g finely chopped pistachios
- finely chopped chives (or mint)
- salt

TO FINISH

- 1 egg
- extra virgin olive oil
- sesame seeds

1. For the filo pastry: mix the ingredients and leave the dough to rest for 20-30 minutes. Divide it into eight parts and prepare the discs for the filo pastry. Form sheets of pastry overlaying four discs at a time.

2. Cut out strips from the sheet of pastry not quite as wide as the length of the cannoli tubes [2a], brush the tubes with oil and roll the pastry until the edges just overlap [2b], then pass a finger dipped in water over them to seal them well.

3. Brush the cannoli with the egg [3a] and sprinkle with the sesame seeds [3b]. You will end up with 16-17 cannoli. Bake in a preheated oven at 180°C / 350F for 15-20 minutes or until golden brown. Prepare the filling by combining all the ingredients, place the mixture in a pastry bag and stuff the cannoli.

4. You can use the second sheet of pastry for more cannoli, doubling the quantities for the filling, or to make little baskets: level off the sheet of pastry and cut out four strips. Brush with oil and sprinkle with oregano. Cut the pastry into 5-6 cm sided squares and arrange them on the bottom of eight upside-down muffin tins, ensuring that they stick well to the bottom and sides, then place a baking tray on them so that they do not rise during baking. Bake in a preheated oven at 180°C / 350F for about 15 minutes, until the baskets are golden brown. Remove the tins from the oven and take off the pastry baskets, then add your preferred filling to each one.

A TIP...

As with all filo pastry recipes, these cannoli are ideal for both sweet and savoury fillings. One excellent filling is finely diced aubergine lemon and orange or wild fennel scented ricotta, Chantilly cream or a chocolate mousse. Whichever filling you choose, remember to stuff the cannoli when you are ready to serve, to avoid them losing the characteristic crispiness.

INDEX